Free to Feel

DISCOVERING EMOTIONAL FREEDOM THROUGH THE EMOTIONS OF JESUS

HOLLY RANDLE SPIARS

FREE TO FEEL
Discovering Emotional Freedom Through the Emotions of Jesus

Copyright © 2025 by Holly Randle Spiars

Interior Layout and Design by Stephanie Anderson
Book Cover Design by Rachel Royer

ISBNs:
979-8-89165-232-3 *Paperback*
979-8-89165-233-0 *Hardback*
979-8-89165-234-7 *E-book*

Published by:
Streamline Books
Kansas City, MO
streamlinebookspublishing.com

To "Faith" and all my clients who helped start
this journey by asking the hard questions.

To my family (primarily my mom)
for encouraging me to write.

To the Restoring Hope Counseling team—
you are the best!

CONTENTS

Introduction. ix

1 Why Emotion? 1

2 Compassion. 13

3 Sadness and Grief 31

4 Marvel. 45

5 Anger. 55

6 Distress and Anguish. 69

7 Peace 83

8 Loneliness 99

9 Joy. 117

Conclusion. 131

Acknowledgments 137

About the Author. 141

Endnotes 143

INTRODUCTION

I **'M FEELING EMOTIONAL,** and I don't know why." These words came out of my mouth yesterday. Saturdays are meant for fun and family time, right? But instead of feeling like having fun, I felt on edge, emotions bubbling up without cause (or so I thought). I was frustrated and judging myself for not having a "justified reason" for feeling as I did. As I mentioned this to my husband, the words gradually pushing their way out of my mouth, I realized I was feeling a culmination of grief, sadness, and hurt. Each one of those emotions was present for a different reason (or several)!

Sometimes talking through our thoughts and feelings, like I did with my husband, brings an awareness to what is driving them. In my case, verbalizing the internal struggle helped me discover what was underneath the surface, percolating in my heart. Though I know all my thoughts and emotions are safe with my husband, I still often find myself trying to "handle" them on my own first.

Perhaps you are like this as well. You want to dress up your emotions and thoughts, only revealing to others the things you've decided are acceptable. Maybe you self-judge every emotion, believing it must be justified or passed through a filter of intense scrutiny.

Maybe you have so many emotions so much of the time that you consistently feel exposed and vulnerable, thinking your emotions are just too much for others.

Perhaps you have a hard time feeling and expressing emotions in general. Whether you grew up in a household where emotions were not talked about, your personality is consistently laid back and even-keeled, or you have assimilated the message that self-control equals non-expression, you truly have a hard time identifying with people who are more emotionally expressive. You might even question if you are supposed to feel at all.

If you resonated with any of the previous statements, this book is for you.

CREATED TO FEEL

I read or heard somewhere that we are *all* emotional. (If I could remember where, I would definitely give the credit.) We are never *not* emotional. We are capable of every emotion a human being can express. And there is absolutely nothing wrong with having the ability to emote.

I think we use the term "emotional" in a negative way because we don't want to truly admit what we are feeling. Either that, or maybe in the moment it is challenging to find adequate words to fit what is happening on the inside.

But we were created to feel. We were created with the capacity to express our responses to thoughts, circumstances, and actions. We were created to engage with others as they feel too. As Christians, we need to remember that feelings are an essential part of our design, for they are part of how we reflect the image of God.

Imagine not being able to feel anything. One would live quite the robotic life. Every fiber of our being is engaged in feeling, both physically and emotionally. Your body feels as you read this. If you're sitting down, you can feel what is beneath you. If you're paying attention to the text, you're having an emotional response to it: relief, confusion, fear, frustration, boredom (to name a few possibilities). Even if you're feeling numb, you're still feeling something.

I think many Christians have shied away from acknowledging we *are* emotional beings and that is a *good* thing for fear that we will look like the world. More specifically, I think the fear is that if we allow ourselves to feel, all our emotions will come spilling out and we will no longer be able to control them—which is a problem for Christians who believe emotions are meant to be controlled. I am sure I will repeat myself time and again: Emotions are not designed to be controlled. However, they should also not be the sole driver of our actions. We will continue to unpack this concept throughout the book.

The subject of emotions in the believer's life comes up daily in my job. I am a licensed professional counselor, and I run a private Christian counseling practice. I have a master of divinity degree with a specialization in counseling, and I have been practicing for more than a decade. During my studies, my eyes were opened to the importance of emotions in the life of a Christian along with their implications on mental health.

I will never forget the client who spearheaded this entire path of looking at Jesus and his emotions. For confidentiality purposes, we will call her Faith.

Faith was doing everything one would expect from a devoted Christian: participating in her church, reading her Bible regularly, leading church groups, and discipling others. She knew a lot of biblical truth, yet her upbringing and personality prevented her from connecting the truth to her emotions. Instead of having the freedom to feel, she thought she shouldn't feel or that feelings should only last for a brief time.

During one of our sessions, I noticed that Faith was more agitated than normal. She seemed confused and sad, but also as though she was trying not to be sad. A thought came to me.

"It seems like you may be trying to be more perfect in your emotions than Jesus," I said.

The look on her face showed surprise—but also realization.

"Jesus felt grief and sadness too," I continued. "Why do you think it's not okay for you to feel those things during an ongoing heartbreak?"

This question led to a road of exploration and healing for Faith, and ultimately, it also led to my desire to write this book for countless others who wonder if emotions and holiness can align.

I have been in Faith's shoes too. I know what it is like to prohibit emotion. There was a natural suppression of grief in my family growing up. It wasn't that I was not allowed emotions, but I don't remember having conversations about them often.

My dad was a submariner in the US Navy. Every time he would go out to sea (for a few months at a time), I would get sick. While strep throat and other infections may not seem like a normal stress response, my body was experiencing the grief of my dad not being present. The pediatrician told my mom that I did not respond emotionally to stress—I responded physically first.

I've spent more than a decade of my adult life pursuing a healthier understanding of the place emotions have in our lives and working to acknowledge emotions rather than barreling through whatever stressors are at hand. I won't lie. It is not easy work! Even now as a counselor, I have to remember to pay attention to and give myself space for the emotions that come from a heavy day of client work. I do not walk this out perfectly, and I do not expect you or anyone else to either.

THE EMOTIONS OF JESUS

In addition to recognizing that our emotions are part of how God designed us, I believe that exploring and understanding the emotions of Jesus is one of the most important things we can do if we want to move from shame to freedom. In fact, it's essential. Understanding Jesus's emotions matters because as the fully divine, fully human Son of God, Jesus provided the perfect example of how to express emotions in a holy way.

Have you ever read the Gospels with the humanity of Jesus in mind? By his humanity, I am referring to his physical responses, emotions, and the overall daily aspects of what it is to be human. I tend to look most often at Jesus's character, miracles, power, and how he reflects God. When I think about his humanity, I typically don't move past the stories of Jesus as a baby.

To dig deeper, I started reading the Gospels with the intention of looking for Jesus's emotions. With our culture's various depictions of Jesus being demure and kind of bland (apart from his anger in the temple), I did not expect to find the full gamut of emotions as Matthew, Mark, Luke, and John describe.

In John 4:6, Jesus is described as "wearied" from his journey. He physically felt tired. *All-powerful* and *tired* seem to be contradictory when describing the God of the universe, but this one verse is so elemental in our understanding of the full humanity of Jesus. His body got tired. He truly experienced what we do, and he gave us multiple examples of how to approach the natural physical and emotional responses of the body.

The perfect Jesus—Son of God and Son of Man—felt emotion and expressed it. Why do we think we have to hold ourselves to a higher standard of feeling and expressing emotion? If he grieved, why do we think we are not good enough Christians if we grieve? If he experienced anger, why do we think it is wrong for us to feel anger?

Jesus had deep, often intense, emotions. *And* he was sinless.

Let's talk about a perfect God having emotions and yet not sinning. Throughout both the Old and New Testaments, countless Scriptures describe the emotions of God and Jesus. Not only are emotions designed and created by God but they are also experienced by him. However, his responses are always perfect and holy.

Because God is the same yesterday, today, and forever (Heb. 13:8), his character is unchanged by his emotions. Rather, his character is often *communicated through* his emotions. Through his sorrow over the plight of his people, his justice, mercy, compassion, and redemptive traits are revealed. Through his anger over sin, we see his glory and holiness. What God says he will do, he does. Faithfully. His emotions do not dictate his rule.

If God functioned as rashly as we sometimes assume—with a hotheaded, angry-at-a-moment's-notice, can't-wait-to-smite-you attitude—we would all be obliterated by now. He does not function off whims and swirls of emotion. He is not chaotic in his displays of emotion either.

Similarly, our emotions should not define our character, though when expressed outside of truth, this can easily happen. Someone who lashes out in anger on a regular basis will likely be known by others as an angry person. In this case, the person is allowing his or her emotions to define his or her character.

Can you imagine running a stoplight because you didn't feel like stopping? (Unfortunately, I do see this happen often.) Even if we are in a hurry, we stop because we know it is against the law to run the light. What we *feel* does not override what we *know* to be best and right.

We also must be careful in assuming we *are* something because we *feel* something. For example, I recently told my counselor (yes, counselors have counselors) that I wasn't feeling very compassionate lately. She responded with, "You are one of the most compassionate people I know! I don't think it's a compassion problem; I think it's a capacity problem." She reminded me that just because I am feeling a certain way that doesn't change my character—who I am.

Emotions are a resource. They are informative. They are a tool of healing. They are an essential part of what makes us alive and keeps us alive. In one day, it is possible to feel every primary emotion.

Because of this, emotions are designed to be part of our human and spiritual experience, while not dictating our every action or defining who we are.

REDEFINING OUR MINDSET

Each emotion has a purpose. I like to refer to emotions as either "heavy" or "light" rather than "negative" or "positive." Most people tend to think of negative emotions as "bad," but deeming some emotions bad makes it even harder to understand and accept difficult emotions. Changing the language to heavy or light may help us acknowledge the impact of our emotions and move toward a healthier place by believing that all emotions are created by God.

Examples of heavy emotions include sadness, anger, disappointment, discouragement, anxiety, and hurt. Examples of light emotions include happiness, joy, calm, nostalgia, hope, confidence, and delight. These are not exhaustive lists, but they give the overall idea of the differentiations. Your first challenge (I am known for giving homework) is to catch yourself labeling emotions as "good" or "bad," or "negative" or "positive," and begin trading out those terms with "heavy" or "light."

Emotions are not perfect. But they were designed by a perfect Creator. I too often see people trying to feel their emotions "correctly" or questioning if they should be feeling a certain way or not. How often have you heard that anger is sinful? In and of itself, experiencing anger or any other emotion is not sinful. What we *do* with the emotion is often what gets us in trouble. I know so many people who either won't allow themselves to feel anger (though it's there) or they feel guilty when they're angry. I feel guilty about getting angry sometimes too. This fear of feeling certain things often turns into shaming or judging ourselves regarding our emotions. We may think, "I shouldn't be feeling this way," "I feel bad (ashamed) for feeling like this," or "I feel so ridiculous for feeling or thinking this way."

I am not a fan of the word *should* as it tends to promote shame instead of eliciting the desired action for change. Your second challenge is to see how many times you think or say the word "should" and try to adjust it. ("Need to" is not a good substitute, by the way.) Ultimately, we cannot shame our way into feeling better.

Let's challenge ourselves to examine our resistance to emotions to determine why we are afraid to feel certain things. Are we scared of emotions because of how the emotions themselves feel, or are we scared because of how we may act? The aftermath of an emotion sometimes feels worse than its initial onset. As we move through the rest of this book, I would love for you to ask yourself a few questions: *What emotions do I gravitate toward or prefer to feel? Which ones do I shy away from? What emotions am I scared to feel?*

Emotions are not bad. They are not wrong. We are created in the image of God, and it is time we realize that our emotions are part of that.

I hope by now you are reading this with an understanding of the spirit of what I'm saying and not the law. Words do not always render themselves sufficient for breaking down the many facets of the soul. Please know that none of what I share in this book is meant to be isolated from the Word of God. My aim is to highlight an important part of our God-given design that has been either neglected or vastly misconstrued in our culture, particularly among Christians. My prayer is that you will know more about God and come to a deeper understanding of how he has created you to flourish in him.

Now that that is settled, let's look at a few anchoring points when it comes to understanding and expressing our emotions in light of Scripture:

1   We will focus on learning to be free to feel emotion, but not to express it in unhealthy and ungodly ways. Emotions do not curtail our call to holiness. In fact, I propose that understanding and accepting our emotions is a part of becoming holy.

2   I do not claim to know exactly how Jesus felt with every emotion described in this book. I do know, however, that he identifies with us and knows what it is like to be us. While the passages we will study may not always elaborate on the emotion ascribed to Jesus, Scripture assumes that we know what the feeling described is like.

3   I want to encourage you to explore this topic on your own as well. Read the Gospels. Read them over and over again, paying attention to and reflecting on the humanity and divinity of Jesus. Fully God. Fully man. See his emotion for yourself.

As we embark on this journey of exploring what the Bible says about emotions, specifically as they are embodied by Jesus, I want us to keep in mind this thought from Dane Ortlund:

> "Let's not dishonor God by so emphasizing his transcendence that we lose a sense of the emotional life of God of which our own emotions are an echo, even if a fallen and distorted echo. God is not a platonic ideal, immovably austere, beyond the reach of meaningful human engagement. God is free of all fallen emotion, but not all emotion (or feeling) whatsoever—where do our own emotions come from, we who are made in his image?"[1]

CHAPTER 1

WHY EMOTION?

BEFORE WE DIVE into studying the emotions of Jesus, I want to use this chapter to provide a little background on how emotions have been viewed historically by Christians, the wider culture, and the Bible. I believe this context will help us understand our own views and responses to emotions and provide a starting point for our discussion.

To think that emotions are a reflection of God is both astounding and comforting. Astounding because, despite that fact, stoicism has often wound its way through Christian history, leaving Christians to believe that emotions do not equal holiness, and therefore, they are to be avoided or tamed. Comforting because if we can accept that God has emotions and we are created in his image, then that means we have emotions too (and they are good).

Perhaps the issue through the ages is that emotions have not been well understood or controlled, resulting in the belief that they are not in line with God's truth. This belief has permeated both Western and Eastern churches. Emotions often get a poor reputation due to lack of understanding, the tendency to consider them uncontrollable and therefore bad, and the all-or-nothing, black-and-white approach many believers often have to life in general.

Then came the rise of emotionalism in the nineteenth century, which essentially boils down to behaving based on how one feels and not prioritizing facts. In emotionalism, truth gets shoved to the side, and feelings become the dictators of decisions. You have seen this in statements such as, "Be your truth," "Follow your heart," and "What do you feel about (fill-in-the-blank)?" Western culture today tends to view emotions as preeminent and uses them as guides for decision-making, values, and beliefs.

With the growth of this mindset, some Christians became even more reluctant to embrace emotion, because doing so would, once again, look like embracing the world. Instead, finding it difficult to assimilate felt experiences (our emotional responses to life circumstances) with biblical truth, many Christians swung the opposite way and chose to ignore emotions altogether.

Neither stance—being ruled by emotions or completely ignoring them—is aligned with Scripture. I mention this because it is important to know what we, as believers, are facing when we have experiences with and conversations about emotions. Like many things created by God, emotions can be mishandled, skewed, and weaponized.

Somehow, in the general understanding of the Christian life, we have concocted a belief that emotions represent inadequacy, a lack of faith, or a deficiency in character. This is an area where I believe American culture has affected our understanding. In the last century-plus, we have seen decades of hiding emotion and then a cultural revolt encouraging expression, albeit usually in unhealthy ways. Because we have seen such extremism, it is hard for the believer to be open to their emotions for fear of aligning with the world instead of Christ. We resort to all-or-nothing thinking rather than taking a balanced approach to the expression of emotions.

In a society that is marked by selfish ideals and immoral standards, it is no wonder that emotions have been misunderstood and misappropriated. It seems like everywhere we turn, messages like "Be who you feel like being" and "You must respect how I feel regardless of how you feel" are continuously propagated, upholding a misguided and sinful agenda. Our culture went from a guiding principle of *suppress all emotions* to *express emotions fully without any kind of truth component or moral code.* Add to that the tendency to label *temptations* as *feelings*, and we have ourselves a hot mess.

We are living in a time when genders are being determined based on feelings rather than biology. Sex is presented in a way that indulges the physical appetite instead of being upheld as sacred. "If it feels good, do it" is a consistent mantra. Instead of acknowledging differences in opinions and beliefs, people are easily offended and "cancel" anyone who does not align with their way of thinking.

We tend to say "I feel" instead of "I think" when the latter is more fitting. Thoughts may lead to emotions and emotions may lead to thoughts, but they are not as interchangeable as we make them out to be in casual conversations. This type of nuance is a small example of the subtle ways in which we can confuse definitions or broaden words to mean more than their original intent. I even swap these two words out when I am not paying critical attention to what I say.

Another phrase often used is "You made me feel this way." While, yes, we are impacted by how other people treat us and it is hard to respond with stoic composure, this phrase gives the other person way too much power. It alludes to another person having *control* over our emotions. Is that really the case?

A theme of victimhood emerges from the ever-increasing emotionalism that permeates our culture. I am not talking about victims of abuse or crime, but rather the tendency to blame someone else for one's personal state of being (encompassing emotions, actions, and attitudes). We are an easily offended society, intolerant of anyone else's ideals if they don't match our own (all in the name of tolerance, mind you), and we are so quick to judge and "cancel" anyone who speaks a modicum of content that makes us uncomfortable. To be completely transparent, even putting this book in circulation makes me apprehensive of the criticism and backlash that may ensue.

Some Christian circles say our culture's problem is that it is driven by emotion rather than truth. But is our culture driven by emotion?

I believe our culture is actually driven by sin, and emotions get attached to that sin or cloak the sin. Again, emotions themselves are not sinful, but like every other good thing, they can be misused for sinful gain. We base way too much on how we do or don't feel as a compass for our lives. This is fleeting and fickle. When emotions and other physical sensations lead without regard to truth or morality, the result is confusion, chaos, and lack of direction.

TO CONTROL OR NOT TO CONTROL

In our current Christian context, emotions are often viewed as something to control. The vibe I get from many of my Christian clients is that emotions are bad and less spiritual than logical thought. Emotions are not considered an essential component of the Christian life, but rather something to be squelched and subdued. There are many Christian authors and speakers whom I highly respect who talk about how essential it is to control one's emotions. While I agree with the heart behind what is being said and the attempts at helping the believer live a holy and righteous life, the word "control" falls short of what is ultimately beneficial and doable according to our design.

This part of the conversation is tricky. There are countless resources on controlling your emotions, practicing self-control, not letting emotions run your life… the list goes on. While these resources can be helpful, sometimes they leave the reader feeling discouraged and frustrated because she can't seem to measure up and get her emotions "in check."

This is where it would be beneficial to redefine what it means to be *in control* of your emotions. The thought that emotions are something to be controlled gets rather fuzzy in interpretation. A better description would be to learn to control *your response* to emotions, rather than the emotions themselves. I think this is where the practice of self-control goes awry. We go too far back and try to control our emotions instead of our actions.

Clients often tell me: "I want to learn how to control my emotions." But part of the problem with that statement is it usually means they haven't learned to *feel* their emotions yet.

An emotion is an in-the-moment response to a thought, circumstance, or image. Trying to control it is like trying to control whether you feel hot or cold. Since we can't truly control every emotion, we end up suppressing them or shaming ourselves for feeling them, which causes frustration at best and anxiety and depression at worst.

Before you completely write me off and consider me sacrilegious, let me ask this: Where in the Bible do you see a direct command or description of the need to *control* one's emotions? Some may point to the command for self-control. However, if we explore the concept of self-control as described in Scripture, we find that being a disciplined person tends to refer more to actions and behaviors than emotions.

The International Standard Bible Encyclopedia addresses the biblical concept of self-control in this way: "Although self-control is not mentioned often in the [New Testament], its several occurrences are very important. Clearly self-control does not come naturally or by hard effort but is the gift of God through His Holy Spirit (Gal. 5:23; 2 Tim. 1:7). Nonetheless the Christian consciously lives out this self-control just as an athlete exercises self-discipline (1 Cor. 9:25-27). There is no ultimate power over self here but only a control granted and sustained by God."[2]

Please do not misunderstand me here. I am *not* saying we are to be ruled by emotion. What I am saying is that we often try to control the wrong thing.

THOUGHTS AND FEELINGS

I want to pose the possibility that the only thing we can truly control is our behavior. Unwanted thoughts pop into your mind. You cannot control the fact that the thought came to mind, but you can choose what you will do with it. You can choose to change the thought. You can choose to process it with truth. You can choose what you do next. I have yet to meet a person who did not have random thoughts come to mind unannounced and unpursued. (If that person is you, can we meet? I have so many questions!)

A line of thought exists that says you think before you feel. This is a very common teaching within cognitive-behavioral therapy. I have spouted this statement countless times. But I am learning that this is not always the case with our emotions.

Yes, many times our thoughts inform our emotions. However, sometimes a thought does not even have time to go through our minds before we feel something. Our brains are wired to protect us. The brain can quickly absorb information and cause sensations. The more the field of neuroscience discovers about our internal wiring, the better understanding we have of how our brains and emotions intertwine.

For additional perspective, consider this: Emotions can be like water. In fluid form, they are not able to be grasped. Sometimes they may be contained, but a container can only hold so much before its contents begin spilling out. We cannot control emotions any more than we can hold water in our hands. When the focus is on control over understanding and acknowledging emotions, we are at risk of heading down a path to stoicism.

On the other end of the spectrum from trying to control emotions, some Christian circles put so much emphasis on emotions that emotions themselves equal truth. In this context, emotions and the Holy Spirit are easily confused, and spiritual maturity is often defined by emotional experiences. This approach is very similar to emotionalism where feelings become the arbiter of truth.

In the emotion-heavy spiritual context, the experience of the Holy Spirit is frequently dictated by physical sensations and emotional manifestations. Worship is an elevated experience. Attention is given to how one feels in response to what is being preached, sung, or communicated.

Services that center on this intense emotional worship can be very powerful. Many lives have been changed through the shifts of emotion that happen during a focus on the presence of the Lord and his power. I have had multiple movements in my spirit that have greatly impacted my life and my understanding of the presence of the Lord. I have also attended services where there was so much pressure on worshiping in a strong, passionate, emotional way that I was accused of not worshiping correctly.

As you can see, our current Christian culture vacillates from one extreme to another (similar to our broader culture), with both ends upholding a false ideal of what is most spiritually mature. As with anything good and holy, emotion can be misconstrued when humans get involved. I am not encouraging or discouraging you to take a side here. What I propose is that we continue to press forward, looking at the humanity and divinity of Jesus as we go and applying his engagement with emotions to our lives.

THE BIBLE AND EMOTIONS

The concept of the "soul" in the Bible (*nephesh* in Hebrew and *psyche* in Greek) includes emotions.[3] The soul is an integral part of being human. We cannot escape it or remove it. The soul is, however, subject to God, just like our bodies and every part of us. Uninhibited and left to the effects of the Fall (i.e., sin), we are prone to acting from emotion, pursuing disastrous desires, seeking our own will, and caving to temptation. Apart from God, we cannot honor God.

For emotions to have their greatest impact, they need to submit to truth. Truth triumphs; therefore, it trumps our ever-changing emotional states. This hierarchy must not be ignored. Does this mean it is bad to feel an emotion that doesn't immediately align with the truth? No, I don't think so. The perspective that led to the emotion may be off, but not the emotion itself.

One of the biggest challenges in our modern culture is learning to view the Bible through the lens of its cultural context. There are many things that do not make sense to us that would have been completely clear to a reader in the ancient Middle East. Methods of communication and transportation were limited. Common colloquialisms and cultural influences were different from what we say and experience now.

Something that remains the same, however, is the human condition. Then and now, we were all created in the image of God. Then and now, we were all born into sin and deal with sinful natures. Then and now, the sins are the same—they just may look differently.

One thing about then and now that seems to be vastly different, however, is how emotions are understood. Rather than implying that emotions are harmful or a nuisance, the Bible simply portrays them as a part of our existence. They do not define us, they're not a problem to solve, and they're not anything to avoid. Emotions are a part of humanity. They are a fact of life. There wasn't a need to talk excessively about them in Scripture, because they were so accepted as a natural part of being a human created in the image of God. Emotions are as much a part of us as the air we breathe and the blood coursing through our veins. We cannot be separated from them.

One of my purposes in writing this book is to provide a resource that gives us a glimpse into what the Bible has to say about emotions, specifically as they are experienced by Jesus. Finding reputable resources on the topic is a challenge; however, one helpful book I recently stumbled across is *Faithful Feelings* by Matthew A. Elliott. He provides a lot of historical background on the Greek and Jewish cultures that were prevalent in biblical times.

Interestingly, though the Bible views emotions as a normal part of the human experience, secular cultures at the time were divided on the meaning, approach, and purpose of emotions. According to Elliott, "Emotions were considered a major topic of philosophical inquiry at the time of the New Testament."[4] As with any study of Scripture, knowing the cultural context of the time aids our understanding of the text. Getting a glimpse of the Grecian thought during that time, even though it is mixed, gives us an idea of what the authors and original readers of the Bible would have understood as meaningful, particularly as it relates to emotions.

The Bible depicts a vast array of emotions in the people we read about as well as in God himself. While emotions are evident in many stories throughout Scripture, the Psalms are particularly filled with them. Psalm 4 speaks of relief, distress, shame, anger, joy, and peace—all in one short psalm! If God were not one to be engaged with emotion, why would he give so much attention to it in his holy Word?

Here is a fun fact for you. There are more psalms of lament (fifty-nine total) than any other category.[5] Psalms of praise is the second largest category at forty-one psalms, and the handful of other categories contain fewer than twenty psalms each. The psalmists needed outlets for their grief and sorrow, and we get to benefit by borrowing their words when we're struggling to express our own pain. To feel so deeply and then find those feelings poured out in pages God deems holy is both connecting and comforting—we connect with the sentiment of the author(s), and we find comfort knowing that God sees, hears, and understands us.

To see that God has emotions is crucial to our understanding of our own emotions. One of my favorite passages that shows the heart of God and some of his emotions is Exodus 34:6-7. Keep in mind that these verses occur not long after the whole golden calf incident. God specifically instructed the people of Israel not to make any gods out of silver or gold (Exod. 20:23). Less than two months later, the Israelites grew impatient while waiting on Moses to return from meeting with the Lord on Mount Sinai, and they did exactly what God had commanded them not to do—they made a golden calf to worship (Exod. 32:1-6). The Lord told Moses what was happening with the people, and Moses headed down the mountain. When Moses saw the Israelites' sin, he was so angered that he broke the stone tablets with the commandments God had given him (Exod. 32:19). Moses later went back up the mountain to have God write on a new set of tablets, and the Lord shared this about himself: "The Lord, the Lord, a God merciful and gracious, slow to anger, and abounding in steadfast love and faithfulness, keeping steadfast love for thousands, forgiving iniquity and transgression and sin…" (Exod. 34:6b-7a).

Did you catch that? God is *slow* to anger. I have noticed a tendency in people—especially those who have a propensity to be fearful—to view God as angry, Jesus as loving, and the Holy Spirit as either neutral or confusing. When asked which member of the Trinity they would go to for comfort, the answer is usually Jesus. Another comment I have heard often is that people prefer the New Testament over the Old Testament because the Old Testament seems to be filled with wrath and anger.

While I understand where this stems from, the more we read the Old Testament with the intention of learning about the character of God, the more we will find gems such as Exodus 34:6. Being slow to anger seems contradictory to being known as an angry God, wouldn't you agree?

One biblical precedent we can pursue in seeking a guide for our emotions is found in James 1:19: "Let every person be quick to hear, slow to speak, slow to anger." When applied, this verse challenges us not to react quickly from a place of emotion and invites patience to the process.

As we explore the emotions of Jesus together, I pray that we will be able to apply the concept of James 1:19. Hopefully, you will be challenged by the Word of God as much as I have been in studying this topic. I encourage you to be curious and look up more verses about the emotions we discuss. Ultimately, my hope is that you will be free to feel in accordance with your God-given design—a design that reflects him.

QUESTIONS FOR REFLECTION

1   What was surprising to you about our culture's views of emotions as discussed in this chapter?

2   What was surprising to you about the biblical view of emotions?

3   Is there a particular emotion that you anticipate will be challenging for you to study and learn to express? If so, which one, and why?

COMPASSION

COMPASSION IS DEFINED as: "sympathetic consciousness of others' distress together with a desire to alleviate it."[6]

Robert C. Roberts draws a distinction between compassion and other types of love. He says,

> "Compassion is the construal of a suffering or deficient person as a cherished fellow... [it] is a form of love, but distinguishable from other forms of love by the terms of its fellowship. Friendship, family, affection, love of spouse, and love for fellow believers all differ from compassion in that the terms of this latter fellowship are suffering or deficiency: the beloved is viewed in terms of a fellow-suffering (actual or potential) or a fellow-deficiency... compassion is not the same as these other forms of love, and that difference lies in how the beloved is viewed."[7]

Compassion is something I have always struggled with and prayed for. I know, I know, how can I be a counselor and struggle with compassion? Isn't that a key component of the job? Yes, yes, it is.

The Lord has changed and softened my heart so much over the years. He has challenged me in so many ways in this area. And I am grateful. Particularly since a lack of compassion is often rooted in pride (and, dare I say it, ignorance).

Jesus is the greatest example of genuine compassion. Did you know that the verb for "compassion" is always either spoken *by* Jesus or used to *describe* him in the Gospels? The word is not used to describe any other person. It is a unique trait depicting not just an emotion but a divine disposition.[8]

Jesus embodied a posture of compassion. It only took Jesus looking at people for his heart to be stirred (Matt. 9:36), and his compassion led to action, conversation, and even grief. Let's look at a few Scripture passages together that describe the compassion of Jesus.

COMPASSION FOR US: MATTHEW 9:36 AND MARK 6:34

Matthew 9:36 says, "When he saw the crowds, he had compassion for them, because they were harassed and helpless, like sheep without a shepherd."

Mark 6:34 says, "When he went ashore he saw a great crowd, and he had compassion on them, because they were like sheep without a shepherd. And he began to teach them many things."

What Jesus saw: the crowds. Why did Jesus have compassion on the crowds? Because they were "harassed and helpless." Jesus loves the lost. He loves those who seek him. The people were helpless to do anything about their social or physical condition, and more specifically, their spiritual one. They had no one to guide them. In *The*

Gospel according to Matthew, Leon Morris explains the plight of the people in this way: "Sheep without a shepherd points to people who are in great danger and without the resources to escape from it."[9]

Before we read that Jesus had compassion on the crowds, Matthew 9:35 describes him going from city to city, preaching and healing. He did not just feel sad or sorry for the crowds; he took action.

Out of his compassion, Jesus proclaimed the gospel. Out of his compassion, he healed diseases.

Tie this in with Psalm 23, which says, "The Lord is my Shepherd, I shall not want." We do not lack anything when he is our Shepherd, taking care of our needs, guiding us, loving us. Consider these phrases from the first three verses of Psalm 23:

- "He makes me lie down in green pastures"—he provides rest.
- "He leads me beside still waters"—he provides refreshment and calm.
- "He restores my soul"—he sees that my soul is harassed and helpless, and he renews it.

In Matthew 9 and Mark 6, the Shepherd who was spoken of hundreds of years before in Psalm 23 comes on the scene. Jesus is the Good Shepherd. He sees the distress of the soul, and in his compassion, he cares for us as a Good Shepherd provides for his sheep.

Learning that Jesus is the only one described by the word *compassion* in the New Testament is freeing to me. Some people are naturally bent toward compassion and others are not. I fall in the second category and have had to undergo a lot of sanctifying work to be a more compassionate person. Compassion does not have to be an emotion we automatically feel, but it's one we can learn from Jesus.

There are several different words in the biblical Hebrew and Greek that translate into "compassion" in English. Two of the more common words are *rāḥam* (Hebrew) and *splanchnizomai* (Greek). A form of *splánchnon* is the Greek word used to describe Jesus's compassion in the Gospels. I am about to go all counseling theory on us, so pardon me for a minute while I nerd out over here. (I love when the Bible shows or confirms our design when psychology thinks it only recently discovered it!)

The main tenets of polyvagal theory, a collection of proposed insights regarding the autonomic nervous system, involve the vagus nerve and how it impacts your body and emotions. The vagus nerve is a part of your parasympathetic nervous system that runs "from your brain to your large intestine."[10] The vagus nerve is part of the fight, flight, freeze, or fawn response to stress. It also plays a key role in the functioning of your heart, digestive system, and your body's ability to rest. In polyvagal theory, the vagus nerve is divided into two parts: dorsal vagus (lower) and ventral vagus (upper). In her book *The Polyvagal Theory in Therapy*, Deb Dana explains how these two parts affect our bodies and our responses to stress. She says,

> The dorsal vagus affects organs beneath the diaphragm, especially those regulating digestion, while the ventral vagus, working above the diaphragm, influences heart rate and breathing rate and integrates with facial nerves to form the Social Engagement System. Out of these biological differences, the two extremes of autonomic response are activated. The dorsal vagus takes us out of connection into immobilization, and the ventral vagus moves us into social engagement and co-regulation.[11]

When threats to our system arise, our bodies may automatically retreat to the lower part of our vagus nerve (dorsal vagus) and want to shut down. This may look like emotional withdrawal, feeling nauseated, having an urgent need to leave whatever situation you are in, and, in extreme cases, passing out. However, in safety and connection, the upper part (ventral vagus) is activated. This may look like feeling a sense of calm or feeling safe to connect with others.

Back to our discussion of the Hebrew and Greek terminology for compassion. According to *The International Standard Bible Encyclopedia*, these words describe how emotions manifest themselves physically in our bodies. The Hebrew word *rāham* refers more to the lower part of the body when describing compassion, though it references the upper part of the body as well. On the other hand, the Greek word *splánchnon* is primarily focused on the upper part of the body, "the heart, lungs, [and] liver."[12]

I find it fascinating that the Greek word used to describe the compassion of Jesus in the Gospels is the one that is felt in the upper part of the body. This lines up with the ventral vagus portion, which is what theorists have found to be the part of the body where we experience true, meaningful, safe connection. And we cannot have safe connection without compassion.

COMPASSION FOR THE HURTING: MATTHEW 14:14

Matthew 14:14 says, "When he went ashore he saw a great crowd, and he had compassion on them and healed their sick."

Compassion compelled Jesus to heal. What is more, Jesus saw the *person*, not just his or her physical need.

In my life, I have been to many medical professionals. Some have provided great care, and others have caused great frustration and anxiety. What makes the difference? Compassion. A desire to truly help and find answers. A desire for the patient to get better.

I have struggled with chronic pain and illness for most of my life. It started with a neck injury at the age of ten, and I have not known a day without pain throughout my body since. At one point, deep depression became an added suffering because I did not have hope for the future regarding my physical suffering.

It wasn't until a counselor challenged me to ask myself what I believe about God in the worst moments that I realized there were some truths I struggled to believe. One such truth was *My God is for me, he is not against me* (see Rom. 8:31). At that point in my life, I believed that God was passive when it came to my physical health. That was a turning point for me.

To look at my circumstances through the lens that God is *actively for* me made a huge difference in my perspective and my hope. He doesn't want his children to suffer. He does not like my pain any more than I do. He is compassionate toward me.

Jesus is not indifferent to you. His compassion runs deep, and he is kind. But his compassion does not mean we will never suffer. Rather, Jesus feels compassion and acts upon it *because* of our suffering.

Are you suffering from sickness or disease?
Jesus has compassion for you.

Are you suffering from loss?
Jesus has compassion for you.

Are you suffering from financial difficulties?
Jesus has compassion for you.

Are you suffering due to the sin of a loved one?
Jesus has compassion for you.

Are you suffering from your sin?
Jesus has compassion for you.

Studying Jesus's compassion in the New Testament and the many miracles he performed as a result may lead you to a nagging question: *Why doesn't he heal in the same way today?* It's true. He is not going around healing everyone today. We don't know that he healed everyone then, either. I do not have full answers for you that do not sound trite. But I believe wholeheartedly that he does still heal. He is still just as compassionate, just as loving. Our physical circumstances are not a reflection of his character.

Through Christ's compassion, he heals and redeems. Physical healing may not happen this side of heaven, but one day it will come. I am a firm believer that none of our pain will be wasted. Our hope exists because of his compassion, because of his redemption. He will make all things new.

COMPASSION FOR THE GRIEVING: LUKE 7:12-15

Luke 7:12-15 says, "As he drew near to the gate of the town, behold, a man who had died was being carried out, the only son of his mother, and she was a widow, and a considerable crowd from the town was with her. And when the Lord saw her, he had compassion on her and said to her, 'Do not weep.' Then he came up and touched the bier, and the bearers stood still. And he said, 'Young man, I say to you, arise.' And the dead man sat up and began to speak, and Jesus gave him to his mother."

Jesus had compassion for the grieving.

Losing a child always carries enormous weight. However, in biblical times, a widow who lost her only son also lost her provision, heir, and hope for the future. Jesus responded to her grief with kindness.

His compassion led him to bring the dead to life! He saw a need that only he could meet, and as a result, the woman's son lived.

Resurrection is not the experience we typically have today. When a loved one dies, we know they are not coming back, no matter the ache within, no matter how hard we cry out to God. Does this make Jesus any less compassionate now? No. I believe his compassion is still very present and real. His act of resurrection to conquer death has been completed. He showed the ultimate glory of his power when he rose from the dead. Because of this loving, compassionate act, we will all one day rise to be with him.

The compassion is there. The action is coming—someday. In the meantime, he grieves along with us. (More on that in the next chapter.)

COMPASSION FOR OUR NEEDS: MARK 8:2

Mark 8:2 says, "I have compassion on the crowd, because they have been with me now three days and have nothing to eat."

Jesus was not a fusser. He challenged religious leaders in their pride, sure, but he did not fuss about little things.

Here was a crowd of people eager to see Jesus and hear him speak. Out of four thousand people, no one thought to bring enough food to last them a few days? But Jesus didn't reprimand them for not being prepared.

My husband learned quickly that I am an over-packer. He has been gradually teaching me the freedom (*cough*, stress) of simplifying packing. I may not pack at a level 10 anymore, it's closer to an 8 (he says 8.5). Thankfully, he humors me by still loading and unloading it all.

As I write this, we are enjoying a cozy time by a fire after walking down a steep hill, in the snow, two kids and three bags in tow. All so our children would be occupied and have their needs met while here. Have we used everything out of those bags? Nope. But we are prepared!

Because of this tendency to think ahead, plan, prepare, and execute, I tend to get frustrated with others who don't—mainly my family. While I have moments of compassion in this, I don't love that my internal (and sometimes external) response is not consistently one of compassion.

Needless to say, Jesus did not respond with annoyance. He saw the crowd's need and felt for them, desiring to meet their need.

There are two implications for us in this. The first is to learn to have compassion for others the way Jesus did. To not fault people for not having it all together. To not fault people for not always being prepared. To not fault people for having needs. And how do we do this? By recognizing we need that same compassion.

The second is this: We do not need to be "prepared" to come to Jesus. I have heard many times from people trying to be "better" or "good" enough to turn to Jesus that they "just need to get their act together first." Jesus's compassion tells us this is not necessary. His compassion also tells us it is not possible to clean up before we come to him. He desires that we come to him to receive his grace for all that we deem ugly and unprepared. He will meet the need.

For the believer, I think compassion is often coupled with humility. It is hard to have one without the other. Compassion involves feeling empathy, love, or concern for a person and her state or needs. Humility acknowledges our limitations in meeting those needs. In humility, we can offer support or resources if we have them to give. In humility, we can also recognize we aren't capable of meeting another's needs all the time.

On the opposite end of the struggle to have compassion is the struggle of people pleasing. People pleasing can look like it is rooted in compassion, but the motives are fear-based. If you are more concerned about what others will think of you if you don't step up and meet a need, you are probably functioning out of fear rather than a place of genuine compassion.

So how do we know if we are compassionate? Ask yourself if your heart is stirred toward the needs of others. Do you hurt on their behalf?

Compassion also involves grace. It looks beyond fault and sees the need. It says, *I am not going to lash out at you because you lashed out at me. I know there is a deeper need beneath the anger.*

Compassion and grace toward my child look like seeing her whining as being a result of tiredness and need for connection. If I use compassion to fuel my actions, then I will pause and give direct attention to her, holding her, talking with her, trying to get her to laugh (because she loves that). Focusing on and seeking to address the underlying need is compassion in action.

Comfort comes from compassion. Do you struggle with giving or receiving compassion? There is a chance that, somewhere along the way of life, you were not comforted when hurt. Instead, you were met with, "Suck it up and deal with it," "Don't be a crybaby," or "If you don't stop crying, I'll give you something to cry about!" When kindness, comfort, and compassion were needed, you were met with harshness, indifference, or even cruelty.

If you struggle in this area, my encouragement to you is to focus on and pray for gentleness. Ask yourself, *Is my internal response to this person or situation kind or gentle?* When the answer is no, it can cause you to pause and explore how Jesus would respond. This can lead to a softening in your spirit that helps you engage in compassion and see others (and yourself) as Jesus sees them.

Now that we've seen the ways Jesus's compassion caused him to take action, heal, grieve, and meet needs, let's take a few minutes to outline some guidelines for demonstrating compassion toward ourselves and others.

COMPASSION FOR SELF

Our efforts to heal are greatly impacted by the level of compassion we have for ourselves and the compassion we receive from others. The "others" part is important because we need others to remind us of truth, love, and grace. If we listen solely to the critical voice in our heads, we will only believe awful things about ourselves, others, and even God.

Compassion is key in how we address shame. Jesus says, "You shall love your neighbor as yourself" (Mark 12:31a). This is not a promotion for self-love. We are warned against being selfish. Instead, I believe compassion and consideration are primarily what is at play in this passage.

Compassion for self will line up with grace. In this, we recognize that our shame is met with grace and compassion, therefore we seek to view ourselves in light of truth. Truth is not bent on shame—it is intended to change and transform. Truth sets us free—it doesn't bind us with shame.

Too often, some well-meaning believers focus more on what they have done, said, or thought that was sinful than on the gospel of Jesus redeeming them and releasing them from the weight of those sins. We are not supposed to be swirling around in shame, focusing on what we've done wrong. We are to be "looking to Jesus, the founder and perfecter of our faith" (Heb. 12:2a).

We can do this when we recognize the grace given to us by Jesus and the fact that he has taken the punishment for our sins. He puts his righteousness on us as a covering. We cannot mess God up! In recognizing his grace, we also seek to see ourselves as God sees us—with compassion. He knows our frame. He knows we are weak. He knows we are incapable of living a sinless life. He sees us and has compassion for us. It is time we see ourselves in the same way!

Don't hold yourself to a higher standard of perfection than God. It is not possible. You will stress yourself out trying to attain something that is not achievable because you are not God. Have compassion for yourself. Know that you are not the standard of perfection.

Does this create a license to sin? As Paul would say, "By no means!" (Rom. 6:1-2). When we have compassion for ourselves—true grace— we see how frail we are and how much we need Jesus. It positions us in a place of freedom to love and show compassion, a freedom to enjoy what God has given us, and a freedom to function according to how we are designed. And that type of freedom leads to more appreciation and love for our Creator who has given us this gift we did not have to achieve or attain for ourselves. That kind of response does not lead to further sin but embraces holiness as a form of worship and gratitude.

What does compassion for ourselves look like? When distressing thoughts of past sin cross your mind, remind yourself of the truth: You are forgiven, that moment is forgiven, and your past is not the truth God has for you to focus on today. This only works if you have repented of the sins. I want to make something very clear: You are forgiven—past, present, and future—regardless of remembering to repent of every single sin you have committed. We would be crushed under the weight of such a burden to acknowledge every sin. But the thoughts that haunt us are usually entrenched in a sin pattern, and it is helpful to have a reference point of repentance. When your heart is tempted to condemn you, either for your own sins or for someone else's repeated sins against you, remind yourself that you no longer have to bring that up because it is done. There is nothing more to do. You have relinquished all rights to that sin. Jesus has paid for it, you have acknowledged it, and you are seeking to move forward.

In 1 John 3:19-20, we read, "By this we shall know that we are of the truth and reassure our heart before him; for whenever our heart condemns us, God is greater than our heart, and he knows everything." Ah, what great truth! What compassion! God's compassion is greater than your shame. Remember that. Believe it. Know that you can't out-sin God's compassion, grace, and mercy.

I would love for you to sit with the lyrics to Natalie Grant's song "Clean." They speak of the truth of the compassion of God toward us. May we see ourselves in light of our Savior.

COMPASSION FOR OTHERS

We can show compassion to others to the measure that we understand the compassion given to us. When we are condemning, judgmental, and harsh toward ourselves, we tend to be that way toward others as well. But when we start grasping the compassion of our Savior toward us, we grow in our ability to extend compassion to others.

This looks like releasing expectations for others. Yes, we expect people to function like decent human beings. Yes, we expect believers to act like they know Jesus. But we are often frustrated, stressed, and angry because it is not possible for every person in our lives—including ourselves—to consistently meet high expectations. Are you holding others to a standard of perfection? Are they never allowed to mess up, make mistakes, or struggle? If the answer is yes, then expectations need to be adjusted. Grace will get you further in relationships than expectations.

In Colossians 3:12-15 we are challenged to,

> "Put on then, as God's chosen ones, holy and beloved, *compassionate hearts*, kindness, humility, meekness, and patience, bearing with one another and, if one has a complaint against another, forgiving each other; as the Lord has forgiven you, so you also must forgive. And above all these put on love, which binds everything together in perfect harmony. And let the peace of Christ rule in your hearts, to which indeed you were called in one body. And be thankful" (emphasis added).

These verses provide a good list of character qualities we are to adopt because we are in Christ. The first to "put on" is a compassionate heart. Notice how the following words on the list tie in with compassion: kindness, humility, meekness, patience, forgiveness, and then love. These are all part of having a compassionate heart. It is hard to fully engage in any of them if compassion isn't the driving source.

For example, I can be a lot more patient if I first tap into compassion. If I pause and consider that my child is likely tired and hungry—and therefore functioning from a place of physical need—I can calmly handle her outbursts. But if I fail to acknowledge her struggles, I will just be frustrated with her behavior. Compassion leads us to forgive. Compassion leads us to love. Compassion leads us to be kind.

Regarding forgiveness, I want to make a special note here: Forgiveness does not mean reconciliation with another person. There are times and situations when reconciliation is not safe or wise. But not allowing someone other than Jesus to have the power over the wholeness of your soul? That is doable. And that is possible through forgiveness.

WHAT COMPASSION IS NOT

Before we move on, I want to offer a few brief cautions regarding what compassion is not and how we can practice it in a healthy way. Compassion is not given with selfish motives. Say there is someone in your life who needs something and helping her would greatly benefit you too. Perhaps meeting her need would make your life easier or you would get recognition from people you want to impress. If your driving motive for helping her is to better your life, that is not compassion.

I am not saying we do not benefit from someone else's life improving. Most of the time, everyone benefits from such change. What I am saying is that our drive to have compassion for others should not be for our own benefit. Compassion has an element of selflessness to it.

Compassion is not the same as being nice. You can be nice to people, but that does not make you compassionate toward them. Compassion compels us to be kind, but just because you are kind does not mean you are deeply moved toward a person's need.

Compassion does not promote chaos. If you do not have the capacity to meet a need, then trying to meet that need anyway is not compassionate. It may, in fact, be damaging to you and your relationships with those close to you.

I usually see this play out in two ways: time and money.

"I told my husband about a volunteer opportunity I signed up for. I am so excited and passionate about it!" Lucy told me during one of our sessions.

"And how did he respond?" I asked (fairly certain the answer was not going to be in favor of her decision).

"He was frustrated. He said I have too much going on and do not need to add another thing. I told him we are called to help widows and orphans, and this is a way I can do that."

"Was he on board after you said that?"

"No. He made a sarcastic comment about our family being orphans and him a widow because I am never there."

Oh, the overachiever with a bleeding heart!

There have been many times in my life where I have been guilty of overcommitting. Dr. Rhonda Kelley, a women's ministry advocate I greatly admired, used to say she was overly optimistic with the margin in her schedule. I have adopted this saying as well. Out of compassion, there are many causes and people I want to help. But I cannot serve them all. In order to write this book, I have had to say no to a few things. It isn't easy.

Money or resources is the second area where compassion tends to get overtaken by chaos.

The story of the widow's mite in Scripture gets taken out of context at times. Luke 21:1-4 says, "Jesus looked up and saw the rich putting their gifts into the offering box, and he saw a poor widow put in two small copper coins. And he said, 'Truly, I tell you, this poor widow has put in more than all of them. For they all contributed out of their abundance, but she out of her poverty put in all she had to live on.'" Jesus was challenging the religious leaders on the motives of the heart in giving, not regarding the amount.

If you are consistently going into debt to help someone else out, that is a problem. That is an overextension of your God-given limitations. This is what creates chaos in your finances and home. Yes, be generous, but only if you truly have it to give. Don't be guilted into giving beyond what you have been given.

My husband is a very generous man, and I have learned a lot from him. I remember one time, before we were married, I sent him some money as a gift because I knew things were tight financially. He turned around and bought socks for the homeless ministry he worked with. He said his needs were met and theirs were not.

He would literally give the shirt off his back if someone needed it. He pretty much always says yes to giving—but only if we have it to give. He always stays within the boundaries of our resources, and it is one of the many things I appreciate and admire about him.

I am reminded of the story in Acts 3 of Peter and John when they encountered a lame man, begging for money. Peter said, "I have no silver and gold, but what I do have I give to you. In the name of Jesus Christ of Nazareth, rise up and walk!" (verse 6). Here are a few tips to prevent compassion from becoming chaos:

1   Do not get lost in the weeds. Do what you can with the resources you have without getting pulled into the details of a problem.

2   It is okay to be creative in meeting a need. Maybe you do
    not have what a person needs, but you know someone else
    who does. Connect them.

3   Do not try to fix people.

4   If you are married, consult with your spouse before giving
    or committing. If you are single, you have more liberty
    in this area but consider talking with a mentor, friend,
    or another person who knows you well and can speak
    wisdom in your life.

5   Keep checking your heart. What are your motives? What
    does wisdom say?

6   Listen and heed the Holy Spirit in how you walk out
    compassion. He knows your heart and theirs, including
    what is truly needed.

We are called to have compassion. We are to be like Jesus and
carry his compassion with us. We have to keep in mind, though, that
he is the only One with unlimited resources. Yes, we have access to
them. But he is the only One who can truly meet everyone's needs.
Because, at the core of it all, what we all need is Jesus.

One final note: The risk in allowing yourself to feel an emotion—
really feel it, deeply and truly—is that you will open yourself up to
feeling all of them. With great compassion, there is the possibility
for great grief. Yet we don't need to avoid that grief or hold back our
compassion for fear of it. We will explore the necessity and even
goodness of grief in the next chapter.

QUESTIONS FOR REFLECTION

1   In what areas do you have a hard time showing compassion?

2   What can you implement to keep compassion from becoming chaotic?

CHAPTER 3

SADNESS AND GRIEF

S ADNESS IS SOMETHING that is "affected with or expressive of grief or unhappiness."[13] Grief is defined as "deep and poignant distress caused by or as if by bereavement."[14]

During the time I was working with my client Faith, her daughter kept making life-altering choices—choices that went against God. She was buying into the lies of culture and choosing a path of sin, much to her parents' dismay. Faith's experience as a mother was heartbreaking.

Faith raised her daughter with the truth of God's Word. And now everything she prayed for on behalf of her daughter seemed stripped away. She was hurt, angry, and grieving, and the experience shook her faith in God.

"It's been a year now since she made her decision," Faith said in one of our sessions. "I shouldn't still be grieving this."

"Why not?" I asked. "The heartbreak is still there. The loss hasn't gone away. Why wouldn't you still grieve?"

"Because I am a Christian. I am not supposed to still be sad about it."

"If it grieves the heart of God, why can't it grieve yours?"

"I never thought about it like that," she said.

"Jesus cried in response to grief. He experienced grief," I explained. "You can't be more perfect in your emotions than Jesus."

This conversation led Faith to explore the freedom to be sad—the understanding that Christians will suffer with grief too and that we can be like Christ even in our sadness.

Before we continue, I want you to do the following exercise. Read the list of words below and write down the first word (or words) that comes to mind for each. Try not to overthink it. We'll revisit this list at the end of the chapter. What word(s) do you associate with the following:

TEARS/CRYING = _____

GRIEF = _____

SADNESS = _____

SUFFERING = _____

DEPRESSION VS. GRIEF

Not acknowledging grief from any type of loss can lead to depression and anxiety. There are too many people walking around suffering from depression and anxiety who have never allowed themselves to truly grieve. I am living proof.

Resisting sadness or grief can only last so long. Such resistance is not sustainable without further detriment to the health of one's body, mind, and soul. Depression, physical illness, irritability, anger, impatience, and anxiety are some of the potential side effects of suppressed grief.

Before we dive into our discussion of grief, I want to clarify that grief and depression are not clinically the same. Symptoms of the two can certainly overlap, but grief is an emotion in response to the pain of loss, and depression is an ongoing, clinically diagnosable response to various physical, emotional, spiritual, and circumstantial conditions of life.

Symptoms of Major Depressive Disorder include extended periods of sadness, difficulty sleeping, and appetite changes, to name a few. To meet the criteria for clinical depression, a minimum of five symptoms must be present, the symptoms must exist for the majority of at least two weeks, and symptoms must impact a person's ability to function in their everyday life.[15] Another common theme that fits more within the definition of depression as compared to grief is a sense of hopelessness. While depression and grief have similarities, the symptoms of grief are typically an appropriate response to loss. If someone is still experiencing intense symptoms of grief after a significant amount of time has passed, then exploration would be needed to determine if Major Depressive Disorder is a fitting diagnosis. In either case, if you are experiencing any of these symptoms, please consider seeing a counselor or psychiatrist for evaluation and help.

A counseling professor once told me that most people will experience some form of depression at some point in life. An experience of depression does not have to be clinically significant for it to still be significant to you. Life can be hard, and our responses will often reflect that.

For the purposes of our discussion about the emotions of Jesus, we will focus on sadness and grief, not depression. Jesus experienced sadness and grief, but there is nothing in Scripture to assume he would have been depressed.

MAN OF SORROWS:
ISAIAH 53:3

Sadness and grief were not an original part of God's creation. They weren't necessary before sin because when humans lived in perfect union with the Creator, there was no suffering. But when sin entered the world, so did suffering. Sorrow, grief, and agony are all responses to the suffering created by broken unity with God.

As a result, sadness and grief also became an inextricable part of Jesus's experience on earth and his identity—so much so that Isaiah referred to him as a "man of sorrows" (Isa. 53:3). Jesus knew the sorrow of death and the weight of carrying our sins.

This title, however, does not mean Jesus walked around in a perpetually downcast state. He attended joyous events (such as the wedding at Cana in John 2:1-11), spent time at the supper table with a variety of people (Matt. 9:10-11; Luke 10:38-42, 19:5), and welcomed children (Matt. 19:13-15). None of those stories of Jesus come across as sorrowful. To imagine Jesus in a posture of depression while on earth would be an affront to his sovereignty. Clinical depression tends to have a component of hopelessness. Jesus was never without hope. In fact, he is *our* source of hope.

What this title *does* tell us is that Jesus experienced sadness. He walked through grief. As he faced the cross, he felt agony. Was he wrong for feeling any of these emotions? Would we judge Jesus for feeling sad or for grieving? Since we know that Jesus is perfect and sinless and therefore nothing he did was wrong, we can include his sorrowful emotions in that as well. This leads me to the conclusion that the emotion of sadness is acceptable to God. The pains of grief are understood by God. Expressions of agony are relatable to him. This means it is okay for us to experience these emotions too, even though we may not always want to feel them.

CHRISTLIKE TO CRY: JOHN 11:32-35

John 11:32-35 says,

> "Now when Mary came to where Jesus was and saw him, she fell at his feet, saying to him, 'Lord, if you had been here, my brother would not have died.' When Jesus saw her weeping, and the Jews who had come with her also weeping, he was deeply moved in his spirit and greatly troubled. And he said, 'Where have you laid him?' They said to him, 'Lord, come and see.' Jesus wept."

When faced with the death of his friend Lazarus and the grief of Lazarus's sisters, Jesus was "deeply moved in his spirit and greatly troubled." Then he cried. The Sovereign God of the universe, in his humanity, was faced with deep grief. A man who, from what we can glean from Scripture, was much like family to Jesus had died. Yes, Jesus had the power to raise him from the dead. Yes, Jesus had the intention to raise him from the dead. But first, his body was met with the intensity of grief and sorrow over the loss of his friend. He grieved what Lazarus's sisters were experiencing as well.

If anyone close to you has died, you know the stunning and overwhelming feeling of the moment you hear about someone's death. Emotions flood your entire being with such intensity. Feelings of shock, sorrow, disbelief, and possibly relief (over a person no longer suffering) come up without much thought. Your brain is attempting to synthesize traumatic and painful information.

Now imagine Jesus first hearing the news that his loved one died. He responded with his humanity and his holiness. Think about those implications. He was not without belief in that moment. He was not without his sovereignty. He was faced with grief and did what was both human and holy to do: He wept.

Commenting on John 11:35, Matthew Henry says, "We never read that he laughed, but more than once we have him in tears. Tears of compassion well become Christians and make them most to resemble Christ."[16]

Growing up, my emotions were not given much regard. They were not shunned or disdained, but I do not remember any significant comments or messages about them either. I do not blame my parents—talking about emotions was not a popular topic back then. Not that those conversations weren't needed, but their importance was not well understood.

As a result, I refused to cry in front of others, except for my family. Again, I was not taught I could not cry, but somehow I adopted the idea that crying was a sign of weakness or something that was reserved for spiritual breakthroughs. (Side note: Now I shed a tear in a heartbeat!) I wish I knew then what I know now.

It is Christlike to cry. If you gain no other knowledge from this entire book than this, I will consider it a success. As you desire to grow in other aspects of Christlikeness—humility, love, patience, kindness, etc.—you may want to add sadness and tears to your list. I am not saying that we should aim to cry every day. But to embrace sadness and tears as a reflection of Christ is indicative of a beauty of spirit that is often neglected but vital to a Christ follower's experience in this life.

GRIEVED BY SPIRITUAL BLINDNESS: LUKE 19:41

Luke 19:41 says, "And when he drew near and saw the city, he wept over it."

Have you ever been grieved by someone else's decisions? As a counselor, I often speak with women about their sadness over their husbands or children. These women long to love their families well, and they see the peace their loved ones could experience if they would stop being so stubborn, humble themselves, and receive love.

This is but a glimpse of the sorrow that caused Jesus to weep when he looked at Jerusalem. He knew what was to come. He knew that even after he faced death on her behalf, Jerusalem would still be unfaithful. She could have peace and protection. She could have freedom. But her rebellion would lead to heartache again.

Jesus weeping over Jerusalem gives us a picture of compassion leading to grief, as we discussed in the previous chapter. While compassion is not explicitly mentioned in this passage, it is implied by Jesus's discourse over what is to come. His love, compassion, and desire to save the holy city brought him to the point of sacrifice. And yet his people were still going to be blinded to the truth. His tears were an outpouring of his love and grief over his people's stubborn hearts.

MAKING SPACE FOR GRIEF: MATTHEW 14:13-14

Matthew 14:13-14 says, "Now when Jesus heard this, he withdrew from there in a boat to a desolate place by himself. But when the crowds heard it, they followed him on foot from the towns. When he went ashore he saw a great crowd, and he had compassion on them and healed their sick."

In this passage, Jesus gives us an example of what to do with grief. He had just received word that John the Baptist had died, and his immediate reaction was to withdraw and be alone. Sometimes in light of fresh grief, we need space. I so often see people barrel through and not give themselves space to grieve a loss—whether of a loved one, a job, or a major life change. Jesus had a quiet grief response in this case. But when the demands of life kicked in, he still responded with compassion. Often, we press on and respond with anger or irritability, likely because we did not give space for grief.

Allowing ourselves and others to be alone, if desired, is okay. However, there is a difference between withdrawing because of loss and withdrawing as a part of a depression cycle. If a friend or a loved one begins withdrawing and it is not associated with significant loss, then my encouragement to you is to gently press in and be present. Long-term isolation is not healthy for anyone. Jesus gives us an example of this by returning to the crowds with compassion and healing the sick.

COMMON MYTHS ABOUT SADNESS AND GRIEF

"What do I do?" asked the woman in front of me. We will call her Ellie.

"There is nothing you can *do*," I said. "You just have to sit with it."

"I don't like it," Ellie said. "I want to run. I want to escape. I want to do everything but feel this sadness."

"I know. It's hard."

"Is there anything I can do to not feel this way?"

"No," I replied. "Avoiding, distracting, and running are not going to make the pain go away. They will only press down grief, shove it aside, and try to hide it. Those things won't heal the pain. Allowing yourself to feel all that you are feeling right now? That's what is necessary for healing."

I have conversations like this on a regular basis. There are not many people out there who *want* to feel grief. In my work as a counselor, I tend to see several myths that contribute to people's avoidance of grief and cause roadblocks in the grieving process. Four of the most common myths are:

1   I will never get out of grief or stop feeling sad.
2   I can get through all the "stages" and be done with grief.
3   I can't laugh, experience joy, or have fun while grieving.
4   I shouldn't feel so bad about this—other people have it worse.

Let's take a closer look at each of these:

1   **I will never get out of grief or stop feeling sad.** I have spoken with people who fear that if they allow sadness or tears, they will not be able to stop the flood of emotion and will become stuck in a permanent state of sadness. To this I counter, *Do you fear laughing perpetually?* Probably not. Neither joy nor sadness can be sustained forever.

There is some truth to this fear. If it is one that tends to cripple you, you have likely been in a state of repression for far too long. Once those floodgates open, you may experience an intensity of sadness and tears for a while. This is due in part to finally releasing what has been building up. You have no framework for expressing the sorrow, no certainty for how long it will last when it all comes spilling out. Scripture promises that we are not bound in this state forever (Ps. 30:5b; 2 Cor. 4:17; Rev. 21:4). In addition, as you learn how to feel and express sadness, you will be able to better experience it for the holy thing that it is, which frees you up to accept it as something that can be helpful rather than only harmful. If this describes you, my prayer is that you find healing and freedom through the tears.

2   **I can get through all the "stages" and be done with grief.** Until recently, the popular approach to helping someone through grief was to address it as six stages: denial, anger, bargaining, depression, acceptance, and finding meaning.[17]

While helpful to an extent, the world of professional counseling is now moving away from that model as it has often been misapplied or applied too stringently, leaving people to question if they should be at a different stage of grief. Grief becomes part of life. It is not something to accomplish.

3   **I can't laugh, experience joy, or have fun while grieving.** Sometimes you need a break from grieving. Yes, the biggest point of this chapter is to encourage you to be okay with sadness and grief. But that is not all there is to life. Too many people feel guilty for laughing any time after their loved one dies. No one—including you—should be judging you for that. Remember, the grief will always be there. It is not going away. As you heal and begin walking through a new normal, you will find the need to have fun, laugh, and seek joy. It will likely not be easy to do so but know that you can.

4   **I shouldn't feel so bad about this—other people have it worse.** Do you feel guilty or ashamed when you experience emotions correlated with suffering? An example of this is, "I am so blessed; I shouldn't feel bad about going through this." But you can be blessed and experience pain at the same time. One does not cancel out the other. It is healthy for us to recognize and acknowledge the suffering that we are facing.

If we don't acknowledge our pain, then how do we expect to experience God as Comforter? How else will we know God as our Strong Tower and Rock unless we need his help and protection? What if, by blocking out grief, we also block out a deeper understanding of Jesus and a measure of closeness with him? If we ignore what we are going through, along with the emotions that ensue, we will miss out on specific points of dependency on God that enrich our understanding of him and strengthen our relationship with him.

FREEDOM TO GRIEVE

When we can accept the emotion of sadness as a God-given gift to express deep love and pain, then we don't have to try to hide from it. We can be like Jesus in the way we feel and experience grief.

Now, I am not telling you to seek it out. As a human being, you will eventually experience some level of grief. It will find you.

Grief often feels purposeless and senseless. Rarely is it welcomed. I think we do ourselves a disservice when we attempt to associate grief with something to be learned. When we assume that whatever happened is meant to teach us a lesson, we add cruelty and harshness to an already painful situation. The result is faulty thinking that sounds like *If I had just learned whatever lesson I was supposed to, this wouldn't have had to happen.*

Do we learn lessons through grief? Sometimes. And God can use everything for our sanctification. But grief exists because perfection on earth does not. When the world was created, it was not designed to be broken. It was pure. When sin entered the world, so did death. We are designed for glory, beauty, and life. When loss happens, we are thrust into the echo of death, feeling all that is wrong and longing for it to be made right. Grief points us to what is broken, which, in turn, can point us to the One who redeems all that has been broken. Ultimately, it reminds us of what is not yet but is to come—eternity with Christ.

For the person who is grieving, life feels different—nothing feels right or good. Meanwhile, everyone else carries on with their day-to-day lives. Even people who may have grieved with you initially eventually seem to move on while you continue carrying the heavy weight of grief. It can feel so isolating.

If you are walking alongside someone who is grieving, keep in mind that many people long for someone to just sit with them. Talking is not always necessary. But it is less isolating to have a person nearby. Presence can be more powerful than words.

Grief brings about a sobering reality that we are not as invincible as we may believe and pain is more common than we think.

Death changes us. Death is ugly, deceitful, and unkind. It rakes through life with its vicious talons, threatening to consume all that is precious. But for the one whose life, hope, and faith are in Christ, death is a turning point, taking us to the glory we have lived for.

Sadness is uncomfortable because it is not pleasurable. Our culture is more interested in doing whatever it takes to feel good and to distract from pain than it is in being okay with feeling sadness. Addiction to screens, food, alcohol, nicotine, drugs, sex—these all reflect a longing to escape.

However, we will feel much better in the long run if we learn to embrace sorrow now.

Some people do not even know they are sad. Part of this is a lack of understanding that grief can come in many forms and for a variety of reasons. Loss is not solely death's territory. While death is the heaviest of losses, loss can also happen in other ways: the loss of relationships, positions, finances, jobs, homes, reputations, respect, and even dreams.

If you are currently grieving (or needing to grieve), what would it look like to invite Jesus into that with you? What would happen if you imagined Jesus feeling the depth of what you do in those moments of excruciating emotional pain? Based on the way Jesus expressed grief and sadness in Scripture, I think it is safe to say that he knows intimately what we are feeling in those awful moments. I think we so often look to God to fix the *cause* of the pain that we gloss over our great need in that moment—*comfort*. We need his comfort in the pain.

Imagine being okay with being sad. What if tears and laughter were equal in importance? Sit with the sadness for a moment. Try to breathe. Be aware of how it feels in your body—the ache, the depth of pain in the pit of your torso. Are there any thoughts associated with the sadness? Are there any fears? Questions about God? Allow tears to come if needed. Allow yourself to feel sad knowing that you will not permanently feel this way. But in this moment, for now, you are free to be sad. Do not try to fix it or talk your way out of it.

As I've learned to ask these questions and grieve in my own life, it has been freeing for me to remember that it is okay to be sad. The response of sadness is good. Likely Jesus would be sad about what we are sad about too. When we remove shame and guilt from the experience of sadness, we can see it as a function of Christlikeness and welcome it for the healing that it brings.

Some losses will always elicit grief. Grief does not go away. It will look different over time, but the loss and ache remain. A longing lingers.

For the one whose hope is in Christ, we can look forward to all grief being redeemed. We can look forward to reunification. We can anticipate restoration. In heaven, grief will no longer exist. We have this hope!

Grief and loss were not the intention with creation. But they are reminders of the brokenness of the world now and of what is to come—unending joy, peace, and the presence of our Savior. One in whom all is conquered and complete. We endure because we know what is coming.

Revelation 21:4 says, "He will wipe away every tear from their eyes, and death shall be no more, neither shall there be mourning, nor crying, nor pain anymore, for the former things have passed away." Hallelujah! In the meantime, while we walk this earth and interact with the effects of sin, let us allow the godly expressions of sadness and grief to cleanse our hearts and remind us of the wholeness to come.

QUESTIONS FOR REFLECTION

1   Are there any common myths about grief that you have believed or experienced?

2   Consider the exercise you did earlier. After reading and processing this chapter, challenge yourself to expand the words you associate with each word in this list. Do you think any differently about any of them?

TEARS/CRYING = _____

GRIEF = _____

SADNESS = _____

SUFFERING = _____

\\//

CHAPTER 4

MARVEL

RECENTLY WATCHED A social media reel of a singing audition and was stunned by the power and emotion in the woman's voice. The entire audience was captivated by her ability to flawlessly deliver each note with just the right dramatic flair. The performance was so moving that I got chills on my arms. I wanted to hear more.

When was the last time you were amazed? What captured your attention, drew you in, made you pause and enjoy the moment? What elicits awe and wonder for you? What makes you think, *Wow, how is that even possible?!*

Truthfully, I had to sit and think about my answer to this for a little bit. I wouldn't be surprised if you do too. We live in a culture of constant hype and excitability. Our brains are so flooded with dopamine fixes that it takes more and more of the substance (electronic device usage, comfort foods, sexual pleasure, etc.) to achieve the desired result. The more we experience excitement over the same thing, the less excited we become.

Take, for example, a fun ride at an amusement park (I will let you fill in the blanks as to the type of ride because I don't enjoy roller coasters). Anticipation builds as you wait in line, looking forward to the thrill of what is to come. You get on the ride, and it goes by so fast that you want to go again. But after the fifth or sixth time, you are probably not experiencing as much excitement as you did the first time. You know what to expect and those expectations have been met consistently, so there is nothing left to spark amazement.

However, there are a few exceptions to this. First, children tend to love repetition. They thrive off it, and knowing what is coming contributes to their excitement. Developmentally, this works for them. They are easily thrilled with the same ride, game, or story. Another exception involves certain diagnoses, such as autism spectrum disorder where excitement can feel safer and more fun in the known than the unknown. And lastly, there are those who struggle with varying levels of addiction. Usually, an addiction starts with an attempt to meet a need—often a desire for excitement or pleasure in order to dull physical or emotional pain.

Drug and alcohol addiction are increasingly getting worse in the United States. According to the National Center for Drug Abuse Statistics, "13.5% of Americans 12 and over used drugs in the last month, a 3.8% increase year-over-year."[18] Regarding alcohol, "According to the 2023 National Survey on Drug Use and Health (NSDUH), 28.9 million people ages 12 and older (10.2% in this age group) had [Alcohol Use Disorder] in the past year."[19] In addition, today we also have addictions to the internet, social media, and screens in general. Research from the University of Michigan found that "an estimated 210 million people worldwide suffer from addiction to social media and the internet."[20] The Center for Internet and Technology Addiction reports, "Over 50% of Americans believe they are addicted to their phones."[21] These statistics are staggering, and they made me pause to address my own screen usage. I highly encourage you to look up some statistics on your own. Doing so has been very convicting. It is hard to marvel when our attention is more wrapped up in quick dopamine fixes than in connection and creation.

I don't think we give enough attention to true amazement, to marveling at something or someone. Marveling is an interesting emotion as it can originate from a variety of sources. While we are often amazed by the good, the beautiful, and the impressive, there are also plenty of times when our amazement may come in response to anything outside the normal parameters of the laws of physics. In such cases, our response reads more like incredulity.

MARVELING AT BELIEF: LUKE 7:9

The words "marvel" and "amazed" occur frequently in Scripture. In Greek, the word for "marvel" is *thaumazō*, which means "to marvel or be amazed by an event or an object." *Thaumazō* is primarily used in the Gospels to describe the crowds' response to Jesus's teachings or miracles.[22] Mary and Joseph also "marveled at what was said about [Jesus]" when the elderly Simeon prophesied over him as an infant in the temple (Luke 2:33). But there are two accounts where this word is used to describe Jesus's response to other people.

One of them is found in Luke 7:9, which says, "When Jesus heard these things, he marveled at him, and turning to the crowd that followed him, said, 'I tell you, not even in Israel have I found such faith.'" Luke 7 tells the story of a centurion—a Roman army officer who led one hundred men—who heard about Jesus and believed he had the power to heal, so much so that he was convinced Jesus only needed to say the word and his servant would be healed. The centurion considered himself so unworthy to approach Jesus that he sent Jewish elders and his friends to speak with Jesus on his behalf. He knew the power of words, particularly of someone who is in command. He believed Jesus to be a man of such authority that his word had power even over illness.

Jesus responded with amazement. He marveled at the centurion's trust and belief in him. The officer's faith was even more awe-inspiring because he was a Gentile, someone who was not brought up learning the Hebrew Scriptures, and yet he believed in Jesus with greater confidence than any Jew Jesus had encountered up to that point. Jesus wasn't amazed by the centurion's faith because he thought he couldn't or wouldn't be believed. On the contrary, Jesus knew some would believe him and others wouldn't. He knew what was at stake. Jesus came for a specific kingdom purpose, and this moment of pure belief reflected the power of his mission. The centurion trusted in Jesus sight unseen.

I like to think of the state of amazement or marveling more in a manner of awe and admiration than that of surprise. When you look at the world through a child's eyes, the wonder at even the simplest things reflects a sweet, innocent sense of awe. Children are unmatched in their ability to be amazed, and nothing tends to produce that emotion quite as much as creation itself.

What if Jesus was looking at the centurion, a created being, in a similar fashion? He was encountering this man's faith and watching his creation in action. It was a full-circle moment. Not only did he create the person before him, but that person realized that Jesus was his hope, salvation, and Healer. The centurion turned to the Creator and put the life of his servant in his hands, and Jesus was full of wonder, much like a parent delighting in his child.

MARVELING AT DISBELIEF:
MARK 6:6

Jesus also marveled at lack of faith. Upon arriving in his hometown, Jesus taught in the synagogue, but the people did not believe him (Mark 6:1-2). He was not well received, and the people "took offense at him" (Mark 6:3). Mark 6:6 then says, "And he marveled because of their unbelief."

There are some people for whom Jesus could literally move a mountain in front of their eyes and they would still refuse to believe. We have accounts throughout history of naysayers theorizing different possibilities for what can only be described as miracles. Yet Jesus performed miracles in front of countless witnesses. We cannot explain the supernatural through physics, yet some people refuse to believe in anything they cannot see and understand. If we were able to explain the supernatural workings of God with scientific measurement and reason, they would not be supernatural, would they? Believing in a God we cannot completely explain, know everything about, or know everything that *he* knows is the crux of faith. If we fully understood him, he wouldn't be God.

Here we have Jesus marveling not just at one person but at a collective group's lack of faith. The people could not believe Jesus was legitimate, no matter what he did. And because Jesus walked in humility and was not bent on trying to prove himself to hard-hearted people, he did not do "mighty works" there (Mark 6:5).

God's heart is for all to repent and believe him (2 Peter 3:9). But he is not ignorant of the fact that not everyone will believe in him, and neither was Jesus. However, Jesus had every reason to be amazed at the disbelief of these particular people as they were from his earthly hometown and would not have been able to miss that he lived a sinless life. For it is before them that he did so.

TO MARVEL

What place does marveling or amazement have in our lives? The emotion itself challenges us to pause and take account of what is happening before us. Our attention becomes fixated on a central moment, person, or thing. Nothing else seems to matter except what is before us. We are drawn in, even if only for a brief moment. And during that moment, we have no words, nothing to make it better or worse. This applies to both amazement by the holy and good and amazement as a response to a jolting situation. There are no words that can be spoken except for ones that lead us to cry out, *Abba, Father!*

Jesus marveled at belief and unbelief. We can too. We can marvel at the incredible faith of a person. Or we can marvel at the disbelief of someone who has seen God work and yet still turns away.

I have encountered both scenarios. My six-year-old daughter, Sophie, prays every time she gets any kind of ailment (mostly scrapes and bruises from playing). I can point back to the day that she began doing this. She had gotten hurt somehow, and our friend and fellow church member Samantha was tending to her. Samantha said, "Sophie, let's talk to God about healing your boo-boo." Ever since that day, that is exactly what Sophie does. And now her little sister does too. I will forever be grateful for our friend's simple act and the impact it has had on our girls. Their faith in God's healing consistently challenges me and brings me to marvel at their belief.

And I have, unfortunately, encountered too many people who have seen the hand of God in their lives and yet decide he is not enough for them. I have had a couple of clients who flourished when they were established in a church community, had great accountability, and were hungry for the truth. But when they started getting pulled away by worldly philosophies and ideas, they became more depressed and anxious. And no matter how much I gently tried to connect those factors so they could experience some spiritual and emotional freedom, they refused to believe. I marveled at how the facts could be laid before them so clearly and yet they no longer had any faith in the truth.

I fear we are becoming too desensitized to what is incredible because we are so often entertained that we have forgotten what it feels like to be amazed. Maybe we are too busy to pause and wonder. Perhaps our minds are cluttered with the cares of this world, leaving little room for marveling at the mighty works of God.

If you think about how being amazed feels in your body, would you say that most of the time it feels good? I believe it does. This emotion, like many others, can occur suddenly, but we can also pursue the experience of it. If our focus is positioned correctly, it is not hard to marvel. To invite more feelings of wonder and amazement into our lives, consider these ideas:

1   **Allow time to marvel.** Get curious. Explore like a child does. Let yourself wonder about the design of a leaf, the way the heart pumps blood throughout the body, or why we have different seasons in the year.

2   **Try focusing on one thing at a time.** When we have a singular focus, it opens up the opportunity to be amazed rather than distracted. Try being alone in a room and pick one thing to focus on. This could be lyrics to a song, a verse of the Bible, a picture on the wall, etc. You could concentrate on the movement of your breath or the way your body feels in that moment. There are multiple options. You decide.

3   **Become an observer.** Pay attention to your surroundings. Not only is this a good practice for safety, but it also helps us to look outwardly more than inwardly in a healthy way. When we observe from the motivation of compassion and

love, we can see needs, we can see God at work, and we can enjoy the beauty of creation.

4   **Celebrate and admire the faith of others.** Be amazed at what God has done in their lives and yours. Pay attention to his faithfulness. This can encourage our faith and cause us to marvel at what God has done and is doing.

5   **Start a marvel/amazement journal.** Write down one thing a day that causes you to pause and wonder.

6   **Sit with the Word of God.** As you read, pause to reflect on what amazes you. (This may require putting away electronic devices in order to focus.)

These ideas are just that: ideas. They are to give you a starting point for incorporating more of this God-given, often-overlooked emotion into your life. In a world full of distractions, frustrations, and suffering, we could all use more amazement to help us turn our minds to our sovereign Savior. Jesus uses wonder to remind us that there is more to life than sorrow. He is all-powerful, and we can marvel at his grace toward us.

QUESTIONS FOR REFLECTION

1   Did it surprise you that Jesus was amazed/marveled? Why or why not?

2   When was the last time you felt amazed?

3   What is one thing you can do to invite more marvel into your life? (And I don't mean in the superhero way.)

\\//

CHAPTER 5

ANGER

I **ALMOST THREW THE** phone. My whole body was shaking. I could not remember the last time I had been so angry.

I am not normally one to feel helpless. I tend to view obstacles as challenges to work through and grow from. But when I face a situation that I can't change no matter what I do, particularly when other people are impacted, anger is bound to arise.

The situation that made me so angry happened a couple of years ago when the credit card processing company that my business used at the time decided to withhold all our funds. They claimed something along the lines that an unauthorized person was trying to use our account. That was not the case, and though I could prove that it was, indeed, our team using the account, they continued to withhold the funds—for fourteen days!

To top it all off, in addition to the heat of dealing with this (the company would only talk to me and no one else from my team), I had to address the issue while on vacation. You may be thinking, *Well, at least you got a vacation!* I agree with you. However, as a business owner, this is the one time a year that I get to truly unplug and not think about work. Small business owners are rarely not thinking about their businesses!

The situation involved thousands of dollars. It involved contacting our attorney. It involved payroll. The hold was indefinite. And I was promised multiple times that we would hear something in two to three days. Those days would come and go, and I would be calling them again. No one seemed to have solid answers, and I was hung up on multiple times.

Close to two weeks into it, one of the guys I spoke with (after having to go through the whole spiel again because you never get the same person twice with such companies) told me to just be patient. I responded with a very firm answer, saying, "Sir, at this point, I do not think it is right or fair for you to say that to me. It is only patronizing and not helpful." He continued to say those things, said he couldn't help, and hung up on me.

Needless to say, we no longer use that processing company.

Even though it has been years since that phone call, I can still feel the anger stir up in my chest when I think back on it. Anger is a very powerful emotion.

THE PURPOSE OF ANGER

Ah, anger. Anger is one of the most misunderstood emotions. It has had a negative reputation for a long time. However, anger is not a "bad" or "wrong" emotion.

Of course, left unchecked, anger can certainly lead to sin. On the flip side, ignoring anger can lead to sin as well.

Anger serves a purpose—many, in fact. It can stem from hurt, brokenness, pain, injustice, fatigue, need, and even righteousness. I believe upholding and protecting righteousness is anger's purest original intent.

Anger is often described as feeling "out of control." It can also function as an attempt to regain control, though it often fails to reach that goal. The out-of-control feeling can be impressed upon us by our environment, as a response to others, or it can come from internal friction.

For example, I go through spurts of frustration when my house is disheveled. My response to the chaos tends to be anger. I want to throw everything away. This is one way my environment can lead to a feeling of being out of control.

Or say you're taking a college class and your professor accuses you of plagiarism. You know you didn't cheat, and you get angry as a result. You feel helpless and, in a way, out of control because of your professor's actions.

Perhaps you believe you should be kind no matter how much your kids fight, others annoy you, or your workload is overwhelming. You value patience and kindness, but the stress of it all is hard to contain. You feel like you can't be as kind as you want. This is an example of how internal friction can lead to anger.

There are various levels of anger and ways of expressing it. For example, you have the person who is consistently "blowing up" at others. Then there is the one who is so meticulous that they get frustrated and angry when something is out of place. These are just two of the many ways that anger can present itself.

As we discuss the emotion of anger, please keep in mind that not only is it a God-given emotion, but God experiences and expresses it himself. And because God has always existed and will always exist—nothing and no one created him—he is the author of every emotion, including anger. He is pure and holy. He is righteous and good. He cannot sin.

As we've discussed in previous chapters, we have to be careful not to label emotions as sinful. Particularly when emotions are a gift of our humanity from a holy God. But emotions *can* be misused by us humans. They can be misunderstood. They can be used to sin.

If anger was intended to protect righteousness, then why are we so easily set off by things that have little to do with right and wrong? Often it may be pride—we elevate ourselves to god-like status in our minds or, at the very least, we think that we are better than others, or that others are better than us (yep, it goes both ways).

Sometimes anger is used to self-protect. It becomes a cloak for vulnerability. Our brains and bodies suddenly think we are in harm's way, and anger is ignited to keep us "safe." This is a common trauma response because the body or psyche was harmed at some point in the past, and therefore interactions with others are interpreted through a lens of potential harm. Anger is attempting to protect us by lashing out, lashing inward (self-hatred), or taking any other means necessary to create a barrier of safety.

I am not an expert on anger—well, maybe on feeling it, but not on all its ins and outs. There is so much to explore, so much to uncover, so much still to learn. While I would love to discuss the biological components, the multiple layers of anger, and the ways it plays out in daily life, the primary focus of this chapter will be on Jesus's use of anger.

GOD THE FATHER AND ANGER

Before we look at accounts of Jesus's anger, let us quickly consider our view of God on this subject. When we expect God's first response to be anger, we have a misconstrued view of his character. He identifies himself as a God who is slow to anger: "The Lord, the Lord, a God merciful and gracious, slow to anger, and abounding in steadfast love and faithfulness" (Exod. 34:6b).

Does God get angry? Yes. But he is not a steaming hothead, blowing up at every turn.

The rebuttal I hear to this is usually, *But what about all the smiting God does in the Old Testament?* Many (if not most) of those times occurred in instances where God's very specific instructions were disregarded and disobeyed. While we may deem some of God's responses as extreme, the truth is that *not* responding in that way, or having a "gracious" response in these cases, would have cheapened the value of his holiness. I have seen a lot of confusion from people surrounding God's anger, with friends and clients questioning if the suffering or difficult circumstances they are facing mean God is punishing them for sin. If you are questioning if a certain situation in your life is punishment from God, then chances are, it is not. You would know because he is very specific with his commands and the consequences for not following them. Examples of this can be found throughout the Bible.

What we find God displaying far more than anger is patience. Throughout the Old Testament, God is patient with his people. Nehemiah 9:17 says, "They refused to obey and were not mindful of the wonders that you performed among them, but they stiffened their neck and appointed a leader to return to their slavery in Egypt. But you are a God ready to forgive, gracious and merciful, slow to anger and abounding in steadfast love, and did not forsake them."

God sent prophet after prophet to warn the people and remind them what would happen if they did not change their ways. He called them to repent. He gave them chance after chance over hundreds of years.

How many of us could wait that long for a loved one to change and turn from their sin? How many of us could wait that long for anything?

For us to assume God's anger is motivated by the same things that motivate sinful humans is to claim God has sin or evil in him. He is holy. His anger is pure and righteous. God's wrath exists because of our sin and his holiness. Thankfully, his mercy protects us from his wrath, but the need for his mercy only exists because of his wrath. Without his anger, we would also be without his mercy.

ANGER AND COMPASSION: MARK 3:5

When you think of Jesus and anger, what is the first image that comes to mind? Most people I have asked about this reference the time Jesus flipped tables in the temple. But did you know that in all the Gospel accounts that describe that scene, none of them use the word "anger"? Jesus's actions seem to reflect anger, as in multiple other cases, but it is not explicitly mentioned that he was angry.

The only story in the Gospels that expressly says Jesus was angry is found in Mark 3 when Jesus heals a man with a withered hand on the Sabbath. Since it was unlawful to work on the Sabbath, the Pharisees were watching to see if Jesus would break the law. Mark 3:5a says, "And [Jesus] looked around at them with anger, grieved at their hardness of heart…"

The Pharisees just didn't get it. As the religious leaders of the day, they were well-versed in the Old Testament Scriptures. They lived the Law. What Jesus was angry about was the fact that they cared more about adhering to the fine letter of the Law than caring for people. Jesus's kingdom is one of compassion.

Like the Pharisees, our anger can lead us to be blinded to the truth. In anger, we can see only from our personal view of justice. The Pharisees were consistently blinded to the truth that was in front of them—Jesus. They were self-righteous (Mark 2:17) and hard-hearted (Mark 3:5).

I have been guilty of this myself through the years, particularly while I was part of a legalistic church. Rules about one's wardrobe, Bible translation, and church attendance predominated the culture there. Sadly, I gravitated more toward the rules than to people. I am grateful God continues to teach me more and more about grace.

Mark 3:5 is not the only time Jesus displays an aspect of anger in response to someone's lack of compassion. There are many other passages where the tone of Jesus's words reflects anger. In Matthew 23:13-15, Jesus accused the scribes and Pharisees of "shut[ting] the kingdom of heaven in people's faces." He was indignant over the disciples turning children away from him (Mark 10:14). In contrast to his approach to the disciples, regarding the children, he "took them in his arms and blessed them" (Mark 10:16). Other passages reference Jesus rebuking demons and storms (Matt. 17:18; Mark 4:39; Luke 4:35-41). His anger drove him to use his authority to bring about peace.

In his book *Faithful Feelings*, Matthew Elliott has this to say about Jesus's anger: "The aim of Jesus' anger was to set things right, it had a constructive purpose."[23] We would do well to apply this to our own anger and ask this question: *Is my anger serving a constructive purpose? Is it serving the kingdom or distracting from it?*

ZEAL AT THE TEMPLE: JOHN 2:17

So, if anger was not mentioned in the passages where Jesus cleared the temple of the merchants and money-changers, was he actually angry? Likely, yes. Every commentator I have read on the subject leans toward Jesus acting out of righteous anger in this situation.

John 2:17 uses a word here that I think is even more appropriate: "zeal." The zeal Jesus had for what was *supposed* to be taking place in the temple—worship—is a more accurate term for what motivated his actions. The chaos of the temple courts being used like a marketplace was highly distracting for anyone trying to worship.[24]

Zeal is defined as "impassioned devotion to a person or cause, which may be either worthy or unworthy."[25] Jesus was protective of what was holy. He was passionate about preserving the worship of God. If we want to emulate him, we need to be protective of the worship of God as well. One way we can do this is by staying focused on God. As soon as we take our eyes off his holiness, we are at risk of elevating ourselves or others instead, which can result in idolatry.

Jesus's actions did not come from explosive, unbridled rage. He took the time to make a whip, which would have been needed to drive out the cattle. He was intentional in his actions and successful in his ability to clear the temple. There is no depiction of harm in what is written.

There is something else to note: No one tried to stop him. The Jews questioned why Jesus was driving everyone out, but no one fought him. Pure righteous anger is hard to fight against. They likely did not defend what they had done because they knew Jesus was right.

ANGER TOWARD DEATH: JOHN 11:33

There is another passage that we looked at in chapter 3, but it was with grief in mind, not anger. John 11:33 speaks of Jesus being "deeply moved in his spirit and greatly troubled" because of Mary's grief over Lazarus's death. "Deeply moved" can also be translated as "moved with indignation."[26] While Jesus's grief was real and present, his anger over death was also boiling within.

In *The Emotional Life of Our Lord*, B.B. Warfield describes the underlying drive of Jesus's anger in this way: "It is death that is the object of his wrath, and behind death him who has the power of death, and whom he has come into the world to destroy."[27] What Jesus did next by raising Lazarus from the grave provided a glimpse of his power over death and pointed to the ultimate destruction of death that would soon ensue from his righteous anger. On the cross, he conquered death once and for all. Warfield continues, "Not in cold unconcern, but in flaming wrath against the foe, Jesus smites on our behalf. He has not only saved us from the evils which oppress us; he has felt for and with us in our oppression, and under the impulse of these feelings has wrought out our redemption."[28]

MENTAL HEALTH AND ANGER

I want to take a moment to address two mental health diagnoses that tend to have a strong anger component: Major Depressive Disorder (MDD) and Premenstrual Dysphoric Disorder (PMDD). There are other diagnoses, particularly in childhood, that also have anger or irritability as a symptom, but for sake of time, I will not be addressing those here.

Typically, when people think of depression, they tend to think of it in terms of a low or sad mood. Irritability, however, is one of the hallmark symptoms of depression.[29] I often say depression can be unexpressed anger turned inward. Usually, if a client with a depression diagnosis starts expressing anger in a session, I consider us to be making progress in treatment. What has been suppressed for so long is finally coming to the surface and can be dealt with.

Men, particularly, tend to present with symptoms of anger in correlation to depression. Poor view of self, poor view of others, and a desire to regain control in feelings of worthlessness or helplessness can all contribute to outbursts of anger and feelings of depression.

An often missed diagnosis for women is PMDD. I like to refer to this diagnosis as PMS (Premenstrual syndrome) on steroids. It is as though the regular symptoms of PMS get elevated to an extreme level. A woman struggling with PMDD will often have feelings of irritability that seem uncontrollable. The best way I can describe this is with a sense of *I can't stand myself.*

I mention this because I find it very important to consider biological factors when addressing anger. If you are having a hard time pinpointing a source for anger (trauma, depression, stress, etc.), I highly encourage speaking with a medical professional and pursuing bloodwork to check for various vitamin and hormone levels. As for PMDD, it can be helpful to discuss this with a medical provider as well and to explore options for symptom management (there is a wide variety, from natural treatments to medical ones—it is up to your comfort level what to pursue).

BE ANGRY, DON'T SIN

Ephesians 4:26-27 says, "Be angry and do not sin; do not let the sun go down on your anger, and give no opportunity to the devil." If you need justification for expressing anger, this is the go-to verse. But getting your anger out is not the primary point of the passage. The focus is on how we are to interact with each other. The apostle Paul wraps up this section with an even stronger admonition: "Let all bitterness and wrath and anger and clamor and slander be put away from you, along with all malice. Be kind to one another, tenderhearted, forgiving one another, as God in Christ forgave you" (Eph. 4:31-32).

Yes, I am a proponent of figuring out healthy ways to express anger. We need to get it out of our systems. I am not saying we should go around being angry all the time, but we do need to pay attention to *why* we are angry. And if it is not for a righteous purpose, then we need to deal with it. We need to address the underlying issues. If it's trauma, seek healing. If it's pride, seek humility. If it's betrayal, seek forgiveness. If it's irritability, seek patience. If it's exhaustion, seek sleep.

As we grow in Christ, ideally we will also be growing in our understanding of what sparks anger within us. The more we mature in Christ, we will find that fewer things anger us. When our aim is Christ, then our aim is humility. In humility, what would anger us is what would anger Jesus: injustice toward those in need, mistreatment of others, sickness, and death.

When learning to respond to anger in a healthy way, one practical thing you can do is use a little psychological trick. We see it used frequently in Scripture (Eph. 4:32, 5:1-2, 8-9; Phil. 4:8; Col. 3:1-2). Focus on the action you want to exhibit rather than on what you are trying *not* to do. For example, instead of focusing on not being angry with your loved ones, focus on being genuinely kind. If I concentrate on how I want to be kind to my children, regardless of their response, I will be less likely to raise my voice in anger. Our motives cannot be for the purpose of eliciting change in others but for pursuing change within ourselves.

How do we do this? How do we become less angry people? Or better yet, how do we become angry over righteous things rather than slight offenses or petty disputes?

We must engage the Holy Spirit in this internal war. Ask him for wisdom, patience, kindness, and gentleness. Galatians 5:22-23 talks about the Holy Spirit actively working within us to produce fruit. It is not the fruit of our flesh or the fruit of our own pitiful attempts to be good. Rather, it comes from acknowledging and submitting to the Holy Spirit continuously, particularly when we are tempted to engage in behaviors of the flesh.

For example, imagine you find yourself getting angry because someone is being verbally aggressive with you. Instead of lashing out in response, you pause and ask the Holy Spirit to be peace and patience for you in that moment. While you may be physically and emotionally charged, the power of those feelings can be submitted to the authority of the Holy Spirit, helping you respond in integrity and truth.

When you're angry, pray for understanding. The more we seek to understand the truth of a situation, the less we will assume. Proverbs 19:11 says, "Good sense makes one slow to anger, and it is his glory to overlook an offense." As James puts it, let us be "quick to hear, slow to speak, slow to anger" (James 1:19b). The "quick to hear" part would save us a lot of trouble and anger if we focused more on listening to others than jumping to conclusions.

Something that helps me with this (when I employ it) is to consider the character of the other person. My husband and my children are not purposely trying to make things more difficult. They are not cruel and manipulative. But my internal annoyance over their "inconsiderate" ways is not a reflection of me first thinking the best about them. When I can first be thankful for them and remember the gifts they are to me, then my heart can settle into peace instead of friction.

A word of caution: If you are in a situation where you are on the receiving end of abuse, or if you have been in the past, thinking the best of the abuser is not a healthy approach. The anger you're experiencing exists to alert you that something is wrong. It would be wise to channel your anger into action by seeking help from a professional outside of your circumstances who can guide you into safety and help you create boundaries to deal with the abuse and abuser.

If you're not in an abusive situation, another practical step you can take is to pray for patience. Has anyone ever told you, "You better not ask for patience because you will be tested"? You are going to encounter testy situations anyway, so it would behoove you to pray for patience! We want to be equipped for what is to come, not stay stagnant in our growth for fear of being tested.

Next, pray for kindness and gentleness. These two do not mean that we won't have to be firm at times. They also do not warrant abuse. We can be kind in communicating the truth. We can be gentle in correcting a highly charged child (or adult). Proverbs 15:18 says, "A hot-tempered man stirs up strife, but he who is slow to anger quiets contention." The best response to anger is not anger. Anger will not disarm itself.

In all your experiences with anger, pray for self-control. I am still struggling with this one myself. I go through seasons when self-control does not feel like a big deal, but then there are other times when I must pray daily for help in this area—in all things, not just in connection to anger.

Finally, remember that "we do not wrestle against flesh and blood, but against the rulers, against the authorities, against the cosmic powers over this present darkness, against the spiritual forces of evil in the heavenly places" (Eph. 6:12). We need to get angry at the enemy, not each other. We need to get angry at the instigator of death, for he is the one who brought sin into this world. Our war is with him, not with God and not with each other.

We have only scratched the surface with an overview of anger. I wanted to specifically focus on how Jesus's portrayal of anger impacts our use and understanding of it because I believe this provides a great starting place in beginning to interact with anger in a healthier way. If anger is something you struggle with, I highly encourage you to seek out a counselor who can help guide you through the ins and outs of your experience with this emotion.

QUESTIONS FOR REFLECTION

1   Are you angry about what Jesus is angry about? Similarly, are you showing mercy where he would show mercy?

2   How do you view God? Do you see him as patient, angry, or both?

3   As you explore the healthy side of anger, what will you pray for this week—patience, humility, understanding, or self-control?

CHAPTER 6

DISTRESS AND ANGUISH

HAVE HEARD THE cry of anguish. It was a mother's cry. The sound... the day... I will never forget. Writing about it, remembering it, brings tears to my eyes and sorrow to my heart. That mama still hurts.

Her son was barely twenty when he tragically passed away in an accident. A mother never thinks that her last view of her child will be in a casket.

When they closed the casket, the guttural cry she gave could only be described as the sound of deepest agony. The sound filled the building. We felt hopeless and helpless to ease her pain. The cry was so thick with emotion, and no one was untouched by the pain of it. Sorrow filled our hearts.

Agony is an emotion we do not want to feel, and we do not want others to feel it either. Unfortunately, it is an emotion we will likely all face, for suffering is a very present trouble in this world. Will it always be because of death? No. The sufferings we are called to are not all the same. We may face agony because of physical pain, emotional distress, loss, betrayal, or other hardships.

We would be naive to think that believers in Christ will be untouched by suffering. While it is true that we will not face eternal suffering (praise the Lord!), we *will* face suffering that comes from living in a fallen world.

Before getting too discouraged and heading down an emotional road of trepidation about this subject, let's pause and look at the example of Christ: his anguish, distress, and love. His purpose can lead us to hope.

THE PRAYER: MATTHEW 26:37-38

Matthew 26:37-38 says, "And taking with him Peter and the two sons of Zebedee, he began to be sorrowful and troubled. Then he said to them, 'My soul is very sorrowful, even to death; remain here, and watch with me.'"

Luke 22:43-44 says, "And there appeared to him an angel from heaven, strengthening him. And being in agony he prayed more earnestly; and his sweat became like great drops of blood falling down to the ground."

Luke's description of Jesus before he went to the cross is helpful for our understanding of this scene.[30] Jesus was sorrowful and an angel ministered to him, strengthening him. But the angel didn't take away his agony. It didn't take away the suffering. It didn't take away what Jesus was about to face. Instead, Jesus's response was to pray more earnestly.

Jesus brought his disciples with him to Gethsemane. He then took three of them—Peter, James, and John—a little further away to pray. I wonder if they sensed Jesus's urgency and sorrow. Jesus told them that he was "sorrowful, even to death," but instead of supporting him through prayer and presence, they fell asleep. We do not know how exhausted they were from the day, but we do know they struggled to stay awake at a time when they could have stepped up and supported Jesus. Perhaps this was a taste of what was to come when they would flee the scene as Jesus was betrayed.

Imagine what Jesus was about to face. Sit with and picture what follows. His suffering was not exclusive to his time on the cross. From this point on, when his spirit was troubled and sorrowful, knowing death was coming, the suffering began. This is what he faced: betrayal by one of his disciples, false accusations, humiliation, being spat upon, abandonment by his disciples, accusations of blasphemy, mocking, being beaten with a whip made with pieces of sharp objects, being stripped of his clothing, having a crown of thorns placed on his head, the crowds yelling for his death. Such cruelty. Such agony. Oh, what pain!

In the Garden of Gethsemane, Jesus prayed from his humanity and his divinity. He knew what was coming. Physically, no one wants to face a cruel death. No one wants to be tortured. Even in obedience, Jesus felt agony, sorrow, and distress, and he pleaded with God for another way—to let this cup pass from him (Matt. 26:39). In his commentary on Matthew, Craig Blomberg states, "Nevertheless not everything that is possible is part of God's will, and Jesus wants to make it plain that he intends to comply fully with his Father's desire."[31]

Jesus knew there wasn't another way. He specifically said in John 14:6, "I am the way, and the truth, and the life. No one comes to the Father except through me." He knew he was the perfect lamb and the perfect sacrifice. And yet, in his humanity, the thought of such intense pain and cruelty coming his way was heavy and burdensome.

Obedience does not mean we will automatically feel good about what God calls us to do. We may face the agony of suffering that does not feel "right." What we are called to do may be hard. In that, we can look to Jesus for strength because he knows what it is like to do the hardest thing—sacrifice himself. Pleading with his Father was not a sign of weakness or evidence that he wasn't God/divine. Instead, his whole being was in agony with the thought of the physical, spiritual, and emotional pain he was going to endure as he carried the weight of the sins of the world upon his shoulders.

If you think about carrying even one person's burdens on your shoulders, it feels heavy. Now, imagine that multiplied by billions. That is what Jesus faced—the weight of the punishment for all our sins. He faced death on our behalf, and that involved agony and distress.

Something we can learn from this is that holiness does not equal stoicism. It does not mean being unfeeling. When you picture holiness, what are some of the things that come to mind? For me, up until recently, it kind of looked bland—stark white, unfeeling, stoic, no fun. That is not what holiness is.

Emotions do not represent weakness, nor do they represent unholiness. When Jesus faced death, he also faced agony. He felt pain. He felt distress. His soul was troubled and sorrowful. It is not sinful to feel that way.

Part of me wants to have you tap into the emotion of agony and distress, to remember a situation where you felt that. But I also do not want to encourage you to go to such a hard place emotionally without having anyone to help you safely walk out of it. Instead, gently tap into the emotion. Rather than remembering the circumstance itself, try glancing back at the emotions and physical sensations. Did your entire being feel wrecked? In your distress, what did you want to do? What *did* you do? Did you feel isolated or connected? How long did the intensity of the distressing or agonizing feelings last? Did they turn into anything else, such as sadness, anger, or fear?

If you can think of a time when you felt agony, consider it a glimpse of what Jesus went through that day. He was about to face carrying the weight—the punishment—of the sins of humanity on himself.

Sin itself was not something he ever personally committed. Yet he was about to feel every bit of its consequences on the cross. Our agony is very real, but Jesus's agony was beyond what you or I could imagine.

Though none of us has experienced exactly what Jesus did, my guess is each of us has experienced agony or distress at some point in our lives. What do we do with those feelings, that pain? Jesus gives us the most amazing example by crying out to his Father from the depths of his being. He was so troubled that Scripture likened his sweat to drops of blood—evidence that his body was under extreme duress. Our bodies sweat when we are nervous, stressed, or anticipating something extreme.

After he cried out to God in anguish, Jesus submitted to his Father saying, "not as I will, but as you will" (Matt. 26:39b). He trusted the Father and believed that the purpose of the Father's will is the greater good of everyone. God's will is for all men to know him. His will required Jesus's obedience and his sacrifice. And that's hard. That is a burden that none of us have ever known—and will never know—because thankfully Christ did that for us.

JESUS'S RESPONSE

In Scripture, we see Jesus respond to agony in four main ways: (1) He prayed, (2) he was quiet, (3) he answered his accusers with simplicity and truth, and (4) he cried out. In times of agony, do we not respond similarly? Perhaps the primary difference between the way Jesus responds and our tendencies is that we may lose hope at times, and he did not. Let's look at each of Jesus's responses:

1   **Jesus prayed.** He met with God at a familiar place—the Garden of Gethsemane. There is reason to believe he went there multiple times before the scene in Matthew 26. He went

to Gethsemane to pray, to cry out to the Lord, and to lay all his agony and pain before the Father. The night of his arrest, he prayed to God not once, but three times. I don't know if he would have continued to pray after that or not because after the third time he says, "the hour is at hand" (Matt. 26:45). Judas, the Roman soldiers, and the Jewish religious leaders had arrived to arrest Jesus.

2   **Jesus was quiet.** During his trials, Jesus was consistently accused of crimes he did not commit, and he gave little response to his accusers. Before the high priest Caiaphas, Matthew 26:63 says, "Jesus remained silent."

3   **Jesus answered his accusers with simplicity and truth.** He accepted the suffering that he was facing. He responded with what was to come, saying, "But from now on you will see the Son of Man seated at the right hand of Power and coming on the clouds of heaven" (Matt. 26:64). He knew that getting defensive would not change the outcome or the course of his suffering. He knew he would not change their minds (Luke 22:67-68). Jesus's divinity held him in a place of humility throughout his last hours.

4   **Jesus cried out.** Luke 23:46 says he used a "loud voice." His final prayer, in pain and agony just before breathing his last breath, was not quiet. Could it be that he did this to fulfill the prophecy that none of his bones would be broken? Psalm 22:16-18 and Psalm 34:20 prophesy about the cross and speak of bones being intact, and Exodus 12:46 instructs that the bones of the Passover lamb—a foreshadow of Jesus as our sacrificial lamb—were not to be broken. For Jesus to yell in those last moments would have taken immense effort and caused excruciating pain. The very act could have caused his body to give

out, thereby preventing the soldiers from trying to speed up his death by breaking his legs.

Through all of this, Jesus trusted the Father knew what he was doing. While on the surface it might appear as though God had turned his back on Jesus, ultimately, he delivered and vindicated him.[32] No matter how difficult and dire the suffering, Jesus trusted the Father's plan. Hebrews 12:2 speaks of the focus Jesus had through the suffering—he endured the cross "for the *joy* that was set before him" (emphasis added). There was purpose in what he did. There was purpose in enduring.

WHY WE ENDURE

Oftentimes, our self-focused approach to Scripture blinds us to important truths that are more life-changing than what we are attempting to find. We are familiar with the fact that Jesus died to save us from the punishment of our sins. We know he loves us. But there is an even greater reason for his sacrifice: He loves the Father.

Warfield puts it this way, "We are surprised to note that Jesus' love to God is only once explicitly mentioned (John 14:31); but in this single mention it is set before us as the motive of his entire saving work and particularly of his offering of himself up. ... The motive of Jesus' earthly life and death is more commonly presented as love for sinful men; here it is presented as loving obedience to God."[33]

Jesus's devotion to the Father, his obedience to his will, and his love for him are even greater reasons for sacrificing his life. He loves us, yes. But he loves the Father more.

God created and defined love. He *is* pure love. No one can love greater and better than he can. He is the One worth enduring for. Our reason for enduring the agony of this life must be greater than ourselves. It must be because of God, because of Christ.

The saints of old devoted their lives to God through countless hardships, some even unto death. They obeyed in distress. Where did they learn that kind of devotion? From Christ. He paved the way for us to find purpose in pain. How can we look at the One who gave his very life for us, enduring agonizing anguish, and then refuse to follow his example when we suffer?

A CURRENT REALITY

As I was writing this chapter, my husband, Stephen, and I entered an intense time of distress. Stephen had been dealing with various symptoms for several months that had gradually gotten worse. Eventually, his doctor sent him in for a head scan. We were called a couple of hours later with the results and instructed to go to the hospital immediately. The scan showed a mass and fluid build up that was putting pressure on his brain. The news was both shocking and terrifying.

That night, we went through a myriad of emotions. Tears come to my eyes even now as I think about it. We were both terrified. Before we left for the hospital, Stephen kissed and held our girls, hoping it wouldn't be the last time. We had hard conversations while waiting at the hospital. We cried. We expressed our fears. We waited pensively.

Stephen was admitted to the hospital overnight. We faced more waiting, more tests, more unknowns. The next morning, the neurosurgeon came in and told us the mass needed to be removed, and he was hoping it was not cancerous. Surgery would be scheduled for the following week.

This information gave us some relief and some trepidation—more waiting. But it also gave us time to prepare and time to pray.

Something unique happened that night of shock and distress. I felt the freedom to feel it all. Any emotion that came up, I thought of how Jesus felt as he faced the cross. We weren't facing the cross but suffering and death were on our minds. And it was only right to face the situation with truth and anguish. Sometimes the only thing we can do in response to life's sufferings is to feel distress and anguish while at the same time still trusting God. The feelings do not diminish the trust, and trust does not have to diminish the feelings.

I had to keep fighting anxiety leading up to the surgery. An image of the surgeon coming into the room and saying Stephen didn't make it persistently invaded my mind. I tried to balance those thoughts by bringing them before the Lord and imagining taking care of Stephen after surgery. While those tools helped, they did not take away the fear.

On the day of the surgery, I experienced a calmness in my soul. I was at peace. My husband was at peace. We had so many people praying for us—and still do. One of my dearest friends came and sat with me during the whole surgery, as did some of our family. My friend's presence was strengthening.

And now, as I type, Stephen is sleeping in his hospital bed, post-operation. The doctor said the surgery was a success! The pathology report came back, and the mass was benign. Now we begin the long road of recovery.

The last few days have been some of the hardest we have ever faced. I keep picturing what it will look like when Stephen is healed—the goal of all his current pain and misery in the hospital. I imagine the joy of having him home, and how he will be jovial, energetic, and able to enjoy life again. But, in some moments, the intensity of the suffering he is going through right now has made me question if it is worth it. I know it will be. But if he knew he was going to deal with such excruciating pain and discomfort, would he have still gone through with the surgery? In many ways, he had no choice. The fluid buildup on his brain would have worsened and caused him to need surgery regardless. He would have probably lost more functioning or been in an emergent state before too long. It had to be done.

There are many times in life when we have to go through the hard to get to the joy. We have to suffer what feels horrendous to experience what feels meaningful.

We need to remember that when we are going through times of agony, pain, and distress. We *can* endure with purpose. We can persevere with purpose. It doesn't take away the pain. It doesn't take away the agony. It doesn't take away the distress. But we can endure like Jesus did—for the joy that is coming. The joy of reconciliation between us and the Father. The joy of the eternal hope that Jesus has to offer through himself.

Jesus conquered death. He conquered the grave. It is because of that resurrection power, that eternal hope that comes from salvation through Jesus, that we can endure difficulty. We can endure those times of agony, even if in the moment it feels like we aren't going to make it.

And for some, that may be your story. You might not make it in your physical body. You might be facing a terminal illness that you know is leading to death. But it is not an eternal suffering. For those whose hope is in Christ, your suffering is not eternal! Your *hope* is. You will experience joy. You will experience rest for your weary soul and your weary body. You have a reward waiting for you, eternal in the heavens. Endure now, my friend. Endure, for what is to come is greater and more glorious than any suffering you will ever experience. Keep pressing on.

RESPONDING TO THE DISTRESS OF OTHERS

Before moving on, I want to add a few brief thoughts on responding to the distress of others and sharing our distress with those who love us.

In one of my graduate courses, I remember the professor, Dr. Nave, challenging us with role plays. He would provide a counseling scenario, and we would have to give our first response. What is the first thing that comes to mind for us to say to that client? These were very challenging situations, and one of them stood out to me. It was based on a true story from the news years ago.

Imagine a couple walks into your office. It has been two weeks since their little girl died after their son accidentally backed over her with a vehicle. The whole family is clearly devastated and in shock. The parents are dealing with indescribable grief, as well as trying to navigate the grief and guilt their son is experiencing.

What is the first thing you say to them? (Hint: Don't start the sentence with "I.")

To this day, I am still not sure what to say to those parents. I would probably say something along the lines of, *That is the heaviest, hardest, most agonizing pain. What you are experiencing is indescribable. This space is yours to feel what you need to and to express whatever comes to your mind and heart.*

Even these words do not feel adequate to meet such pain. But I know what *not* to say.

When facing the greatest, most distressing time of his life, no one told Jesus, *It will be all right.* No one told him to just think positively in the face of suffering and death. Jesus did not say those platitudes to others either.

Jesus wept. He cried out. He expressed his pain. How do you think you would have responded to him in those moments? Would you have been uncomfortable? Would you have wanted him to stop? Would you have tried to get him to look on the bright side?

Instead, what if you asked if you could embrace him? What if you said, "I don't have words but let me pray with you, Jesus"? What if you tried to feel what he was feeling instead of being uncomfortable with it?

During this season when our lives have been turned upside down, Stephen and I have been overwhelmed (in a good way) with the support of our community. From the moment we found out about the brain mass, we decided we would not be private about what we were facing. It is the best decision we have made through this.

We have had multiple people reaching out to us. Friends and family have prayed with us, sat with us, and cried with us. We've had friends tell us they don't have words—and we don't either. I appreciate their honesty and their presence. It is okay for all of us to be in shock.

I had a friend boldly say that she knows I am facing my greatest fear—loss—and remind me that, even in that, God is sovereign. Do you know how I felt in response to that? I felt known. She knows me well enough to know my greatest fear, call it out, and remind me of the truth. It was anchoring to my soul. If an acquaintance had said that, it probably wouldn't have come across as so deeply poignant.

If you are in agony, express it. Let others in on your pain. Remember there is a difference between complaining and speaking a reality that invites conversation and hope. Surround yourself with people who love you, support you, and care about you—and you, them.

When you find yourself in the position of being the support person to someone who is suffering, don't worry about what to say or not to say. Pray for wisdom. Seek to love your person well. Honor them in your conversation. Be kind. Pray for them. Pray *with* them. Sit with them. Do their dishes. Text them to check in. Don't use the excuse of "they may not want to talk." Be willing to let them decide if they want to talk or not. This is not a time to be easily offended.

And if you are the one needing support, receive it. If someone offers to help, take it. If they offer to bring you food or be present with you, say yes. By saying yes to help, you are also saying yes to being served by the body of Christ. You are receiving precious gifts of connection. Keep in mind that in order to give and receive this kind of support, you must build relationships over time, and you have to be open and honest about your needs. By doing this, you will also realize that you are not alone. Allow yourself to be surrounded by your community of people who love you.

QUESTIONS FOR REFLECTION

1   In times of distress, anguish, or anxiety, do you turn toward God or away from him? Do you believe he will comfort you?

2   Do you invite others into distress and anguish in a healthy way to support, encourage, and pray with you? If not, what's one step you can take to let someone else know what you need?

\\//

CHAPTER 7

PEACE

SAIAH 32:17 SAYS, "And the effect of righteousness will be peace, and the result of righteousness, quietness and trust forever." Peace. The ever-elusive state of being for those who have not yet experienced it. And for those who have, they want to keep it and guard it.

The battle for peace is real. Those dealing with depression or anxiety (or both), for example, may think that peace is unattainable. How long you have been dealing with those diagnoses can greatly determine your thoughts on peace. Some people long for peace and are fighting for it so much, but the struggle is getting greater rather than easier. Others have been without peace for so long that they no longer think it is possible to experience it.

I reached out to several friends and colleagues to get their take on how they would describe peace. Here's what they had to say:

- "For me, peace doesn't mean an absence of activity or chaos, but an inner steadiness in the midst of chaos. I think of the word 'stillness' when I think of peace."

- "Peace—an inner contentment or acceptance. A deeply comforting feeling that everything will be okay."
- "It does not mean to be in a place where there is no noise, trouble, or hard work. It means to be in the midst of those things and still be calm in your heart."
- "For me, it's nature. I love being outside and seeing all that God has created around us. Going on hikes to clear my mind and get that tranquility."
- "I feel like in my experience there are two types of peace: spiritual and physical. When I experience spiritual peace, it is a true and solid trust that the Lord is in control (of whatever circumstance I am anxious about or just in general), so I am able to rest in his provision and his presence. Then there is physical peace, which honestly is harder to nail down because it involves various aspects of my daily life. I have recently realized that I am most at peace when I am with my husband and able to share some of my daily burdens with him (caring for our baby, thinking about meals, managing our home, etc.) and also just relax in his presence. In a way, this is just an example of the larger role God plays as he ultimately carries our burdens and provides for our needs and allows us to rest in relationship with him without fear of shame or hurt."

How would you describe peace? What would you add to this list?

JESUS OUR PEACE: EPHESIANS 2:13-17

Up until now, we have been focusing primarily on the emotions of Jesus. This chapter is a little different in that, instead of focusing on something Jesus experienced as a human, we are focusing on what he offers *to* us as humans. *He* is peace. He defines it. He extends it. He is the source of it. So to say Jesus felt peace while on earth is an understatement.

The Gospels do not specifically point to peace as an emotion Jesus expressed. However, Ephesians 2:13-17 says this:

> But now in Christ Jesus you who once were far off have been brought near by the blood of Christ. For he himself is our peace, who has made us both one and has broken down in his flesh the dividing wall of hostility by abolishing the law of commandments expressed in ordinances, that he might create in himself one new man in place of the two, so making peace, and might reconcile us both to God in one body through the cross, thereby killing the hostility. And he came and preached peace to you who were far off and peace to those who were near.

Jesus came to the earth to bring peace. While we tend to think of peace in an emotional sense, there is a large spiritual component to it that goes beyond us as individuals. When we think of peace under its definition as the cessation of war, that is ultimately what Christ came to do. The war with the enemy is won through Jesus. The knowledge that the enemy cannot and will not win the ongoing fight brings peace to our battle-worn souls.

The primary message of the gospel is peace. Jesus offers to settle the war in our souls—the one that rages with sin, the flesh, and the worries of the world.

The resurrection is a great reminder that we can have a solid hope and an anchoring peace, for the One who conquered death is the same One who provides peace. He is the One who reassures our hearts before him. He is the One who holds all things, knows all things, and provides all things. It is to the resurrected King that we surrender and say, "I am miserable and floundering without you."

Peace is available. We have only to fix our eyes on Jesus. When our focus is on the One who is sovereign, who is greater and more powerful than anyone and anything, then our hearts can rest in the peace that comes through Christ Jesus himself. He offers us *himself.*

I think we often want the benefits of Christ without wanting *him.* As a human and as God, he is the One we should want. He is to be desired, cherished, and sought after. You want love? Seek Jesus. You want rest? Seek Jesus. You want wisdom? Seek Jesus. You want peace? Seek Jesus.

Isaiah 26:3-4 says, "You keep him in perfect peace whose mind is stayed on you, because he trusts in you. Trust in the Lord forever, for the Lord God is an everlasting rock."

We are promised peace by the most powerful One in the universe, the One who *created* the universe. And yet we so often set our sights on our ideal life and strive for peace in our own way rather than focusing on the Creator who knows all things. We trust in our version of "God," who is often just a more powerful prototype of ourselves, instead of in the God who created all and is over all. No wonder we have a hard time finding peace.

God is all about words. The Bible begins with him creating with words. He spoke and the sun, so hot no one could come close to touching it, came into existence. The galaxies that extend beyond what the human eye can see were spoken into being. Perfect order and harmony came alive by his voice. Words are important. Words are powerful.

The perfect, holy, loving, righteous God speaks truth and only truth. He does not and cannot lie. His Word is true. It is futile to contest it. We may not fully understand his Word, but we can rest in the confidence that he is good, right, and true.

What does this have to do with peace? Well, what tends to prevent us from pursuing and experiencing peace are words. Mainly, our own words. Words that infiltrate our minds on such a repeated loop that we automatically assume they are true simply because we thought them. After all, who wants to call themselves a liar?

ANXIETY

That never-ending string of words that runs through our brains has a name: anxiety. Anxiety can have many sources, but a common one for many people is death.

We are scared of loss and what may happen to us or someone else. Jesus faced death. I want to make something very clear though. Jesus was not anxious. Anxiety is a reaction to the unknown, with a mixture of anticipation and fear of what could happen. Jesus knew what was going to happen, and he knew that there was great purpose to what he was about to go through. He trusted his Father completely. But in his humanity, he did not want to experience the pain. As he was facing the reality of a cruel cross, he experienced anguish, but he did not suffer anxiety. Most of us will experience some measure of anxiety in our lifetimes. From fleeting moments of panic to nervousness to fear that grips your chest and refuses to let go, the levels vary. We are not all-knowing, and anxiety reminds us of this fact.

But God is all-knowing. He does not fear the future. He knows exactly what will happen. And he is the only One who can handle that kind of information. Humanity has proven time and time again that we are not good at trying to be God. Our attempts never turn out well.

I wonder, though, if we sometimes question whether God is good at being God. So many bad things happen in this world. For a time, we can tolerate them. But when those bad things hit home, we question God. We wonder if he can be trusted. We wonder how he can be good when life is so painful.

The more we question his goodness in his sovereignty, the less likely we will be to trust him with anything, particularly the future.

Anxiety likes to play out the worst-case scenarios. Shortly after my oldest was born, I remember driving down the road and an image flashed through my mind. There was nothing specific that led to this thought. I was not thinking about death at the time. But the image was of my husband and my daughter standing at my grave. The thought made me want to cry but scared me at the same time.

I have always been a very visual person, so most anxious thoughts play like movie scenes in my mind. They look real.

Some people think without imagery attached. Some have physical sensations more than specific thoughts. Regardless of how we think and process, our brains and bodies will respond to our surroundings. If we are not conditioning our brains with truth, then we will continue to succumb to anxiety.

Here are a few things to keep in mind when it comes to anxiety. The first is that multiple emotions, sensations, and responses get lumped into a broad definition of anxiety. For example, anxiety and fear often get so intertwined that people don't always know the difference between the two. But unlike anxiety, there are healthy, God-given fears that help protect us, and there is no way that we could avoid feeling fear in some situations unless we were God himself.

I will give you an example. An instinctive fear of present danger is initiated in our bodies to protect us from harm. When my daughter, Sophie, was a toddler, she chased our dog into the street. They both got away from me so quickly, and I could hardly catch up. As she was running closer and closer to danger and I was yelling for her to stop, sheer panic coursed through my body. I was terrified. I heard and saw a car approaching. Thankfully, it was my neighbor and she was paying attention, so she was able to stop in time. No one was hurt, but that was the most terrifying experience of my life. My body still feels like the air is getting sucked out of me when I think about that moment.

The fear that came with that experience led to action. I was running as quickly as I could and shouting as loudly as possible. God has designed us with instincts that protect us and keep us alive. This type of fear is natural and good, and it helps us respond to immediate danger.

We have to give special attention to discern between what is anxious thinking, a trauma response, and legitimate danger. If we do not, then we risk misusing Scripture by trying to provide an answer or a quick fix for something that is trying to tell us an entirely different message. Emotions are informative. Anxiety could be providing multiple messages of danger, concern, lack, or fear.

There is another aspect of anxiety that I want to call out. Yes, your anxious thoughts could happen and could be true. That's what is so distressing and tricky about anxiety—in most cases, what you are thinking *could* happen. You are right. The same protective capacity in our brains that helps keep us alive also tries to prevent harm and plan for what may happen.

But here is what we miss out on when we're so focused on what is to come: the present. We miss out on present joy. We miss out on the fact that whatever we are thinking might happen is not what is happening right now. By buying into and believing the anxious thoughts, we are robbing ourselves of experiences and peace in the present.

FOCUS TOOLS

So, how do we move through anxiety to find peace? There are multiple methods to combat anxiety, but I want to share with you two of my favorites that I personally use and have encouraged others to use as well.

The first is what I call the Philippians 4:8 list. Paul gives us a great example of what to concentrate on instead of our anxious thoughts. He gives a prescription of where to turn our minds. Most of us have heard this verse countless times as a response to anxiety. But often it gets put in a poetic position in our minds, and we rarely actually use it. This list helps put it into practice. Try turning each adjective in this verse into a category, and then write down the first thing that comes to mind when you think of each one:

TRUE = _____

HONORABLE = _____

JUST = _____

PURE = _____

LOVELY = _____

COMMENDABLE = _____

EXCELLENT/PRAISEWORTHY = _____

Do you have a positive experience with what you wrote down? Can you spend time thinking about that?

For example, for "honorable" I wrote down the military. I have a lot of experience with this because I grew up in a military family. I have plenty of memories I could spend hours thinking about if I wanted. But your experience with the military might be different than mine, so that example might not work the same for you. You may not be able to come up with something for each category and that is okay. The goal is to write down something you have had good experiences with and could spend time thinking about.

My encouragement to you is to put your list on a notecard to keep in your pocket or somewhere on your phone—anywhere you can easily access it. You will be more likely to use the list in times of anxious thinking if it is nearby. Feel free to add or remove items from your list at any point. It is for your benefit, so you can adjust it as needed. The more time you spend thinking about the good things on your list, the less time you will have to think of your anxious thoughts.

The second activity I like to use (I use "like" loosely as this one can be very difficult at times) is what I call "Even if, he is." Play out the worst-case scenario in your mind. If you are lingering with a question, go ahead and make it a scenario instead. Questions about the unknown breed anxiety. Once you play out the scenario, say how you would feel if that happened (for example: hurt, sad, angry, or devastated). The next part is probably the most challenging. State who God will still be *even if* your worst-case scenario happens. Speak this truth to your heart over and over. Confess to God that you really do not want that to happen—you don't want to go through the pain and agony that your scenario would bring. Then settle your heart with the confession of who he is—always. Who he is now is who he will be then too.

JESUS ABOVE ALL ELSE

Jesus told his disciples, "Peace I leave with you; my peace I give to you. Not as the world gives do I give to you. Let not your hearts be troubled, neither let them be afraid" (John 14:27) and "I have said these things to you, that in me you may have peace. In the world you will have tribulation. But take heart; I have overcome the world" (John 16:33).

True, lasting peace is only found in Jesus. But *how* is it found in him? While you cannot self-generate peace, I do believe a shift in focus is necessary to experience it. Peace comes through agreeing with the truth that Jesus says—about himself, you, and your circumstances—and acting upon or resting in that truth.

For example, imagine you recently bought a house. You make just enough to live on, and you unexpectedly get laid off from your job—one that you were dedicated to and worked very hard at. Your severance may cover a month's worth of expenses. You are left in a whirlwind of distress, uncertainty, fear, grief, and anger. What do you do?

This scenario happened to me. It left me reeling. I was so shocked, confused, and hurt. But I had been praying for a sabbatical, a time to rest. This was not exactly the way that I saw that playing out, but the Lord provided what I needed. He challenged me to trust him to be faithful and to provide.

So I did.

There was so much peace in trusting God to take care of me during those next few months. Instead of hunting for another job, I believed he was directing me to focus on private practice work in counseling. I had been doing that on the side for a few years, but now it was time to make it happen full time. (Side note: It usually takes a few years to build to full-time private practice.)

On paper, nothing made sense financially that year. But somehow, I never missed a mortgage payment. I had so many friends volunteering to do things for me—build a website, take professional headshots, take me to a concert—that each encounter felt like another gift from the Lord through his people. Financially, it was the hardest year. Emotionally and spiritually, it was the best year because of the peace that came with trusting the Lord to take care of me. I started looking forward to how he would provide.

Peace did not come through the circumstances. Peace came through believing with much hope that God was going to take care of me. I was single and lived alone. It is not fun to have a sporadic income. But God kept reminding me to trust him with every work provision, every financial provision, and every gift. What seemed like such a devastating event in my life turned into one that promoted the most peace.

CONFESSION

Peace—or the lack thereof—not only impacts us individually but also relationally. There are three primary and crucial ways of seeking peace when it comes to our relationship with God and with others: confession, confrontation, and worship.

Confession is cleansing, healing, and necessary. Confession can also be incredibly challenging. We can be challenged by the act of confessing, knowing what to confess, and wondering how the recipient will respond.

Romans 10:9 says that we are to "confess with [our] mouths that Jesus is Lord" to receive salvation. Salvation initiates and confirms eternal peace.

When we confess our sin before God, we acknowledge that what we did was an offense to him and hurt our relational connection. Whether we feel fear or peace as we confess our sins depends on our view of God. If we see him as only holy and just, we may conclude that he will respond to our confession in a jealous rage. But if we remember that he is also merciful, faithful, and compassionate, then we can come before him grieved by our sin but desiring his help and cleansing power. From this vantage point, we can experience peace.

When we confess our sins to each other, as we are instructed to do (James 5:16), we invite honesty and deep connection through our vulnerability. Is it easy to confess? No, not initially. But as you grow spiritually and in the practice of confession, you will begin to see how healing and encouraging confession can be when met with compassion rather than shame. (Shame is what we often naturally anticipate in confession.) Our sins impact each other, and therefore confession does as well. When in fellowship with other believers who are seeking Christ and seeking peace, confession becomes a crucial part of that bond, upholding genuine peace.

CONFRONTATION

Similar to confession, healthy confrontation can also encourage peace. We need to confront our own sin to create room and opportunity for peace. We often have to address the sin of others too.

However, confrontation is not always sin-related. Oftentimes there are merely differences in opinions, perspectives, and assumptions that are helpful to address. If we avoid confrontation and allow things to go unspoken, we can end up making assumptions that are not true.

For example, a few years ago, a coworker of mine made a comment in passing to other coworkers. At the time, I was not sure if he was being genuine or sarcastic. If genuine, it was a very kind and encouraging comment. If sarcastic, well, it was the complete opposite. I had not been working with him long enough to know the difference. I later processed the comment, reflected on the situation, and decided to ask him about it. He confirmed that he was being genuine and expounded on his comment further. There was nothing tense about our conversation (albeit I was nervous to approach the subject). The conversation promoted peace because we were able to be honest and kind in the process.

Had I not addressed this with him early on, I would have consistently questioned our interactions. But that conversation clarified his purpose and revealed his character in a good way.

Does this mean you need to go around confronting every situation where an assumption has been made? Absolutely not! For some, "assumption" is their middle name! Assess with facts and truth as much as possible and see if you can come to a resolution first. Speak with God about it. If the relationship between you and that other person will be harmed or impacted by remaining quiet and not talking about it, then you will likely need to have a conversation with that person.

Here is another tip to keep in mind, one that I use and share with my clients frequently. Ask yourself this, *What are my assumptions saying about this person's character?* If you are honest with your answer, that one question can provide a quick adjustment to your assumptions and potentially obliterate them.

Consider these examples. Your spouse is quiet. You assume he is mad at you, but you have no idea why. The reality is he has had a very stressful day and is in a state of overwhelm. He is not mad at you; he has simply reached a limit on his processing capacity for the day.

You send a lengthy text message to a friend. Her response is much shorter than what you expected. You assume that you said too much, and she is irritated with you. The reality is that her kids distracted her in the middle of reading your text, and she only had enough time to respond briefly.

In the first scenario, the assumption says of your spouse's character that he is angry, passive, and unkind. In the second scenario, the assumption says of your friend's character that she is dismissive and easily annoyed. Are those assumptions true of each person's character?

There is a caveat to this. There are plenty of people out there who are passive-aggressive, defensive, and unapproachable. If this is *consistently* how they act, then it may be a reflection of their character. You need to seek wisdom, caution, and likely professional help to determine if confrontation will be beneficial. (A great resource to help evaluate such situations is the book *When to Walk Away* by Gary Thomas.)

WORSHIP

Lastly, we also experience peace when we worship. Worship sets the tone for aligning our hearts and minds with truth.

Sunday mornings are a welcoming reset and challenge to jumpstart the week. Hearing the gospel preached reminds me what I'm hungry for. Singing songs of worship reminds me of God's faithfulness and mercy. It is hard to worry in this setting if my mind is truly focused on the words and my heart is postured to learn.

Though so vital to our overall spiritual health, it is often a battle in my family to get to church (particularly on time). This morning, for example, we had to do outfit changes with the girls due to spills as well as another diaper change. They did not want to brush their teeth. Neither my husband nor I felt very good due to lingering health challenges. But we made it.

As I sat in service, God so kindly reminded me that it is good to be in the house of the Lord and to sing praises to him (Ps. 26:8, 27:4, 147:1). The sermon was convicting. We were led to a time of quiet confession before God, and the Holy Spirit revealed to me a sin of unforgiveness I had been hanging on to that was impacting my peace. And then we sang of the wondrous cross.

I wish I could tell you that the rest of the day was blissfully peaceful. It wasn't. The day was challenging for multiple reasons. But I love that the Holy Spirit kept reminding me of the sermon. I love that he kept encouraging me to respond differently.

And that is what corporate worship can do. It reminds us of truth and that we are not the only ones seeking to pursue Christ. For the body of Christ, unique and different as we all are, to come together and agree in worship that God is who he says he is—that is powerful. And it promotes peace to affirm our beliefs together. We get to help carry one another's beliefs and burdens.

Americans have bought into an isolating approach to strength. The encouragement to "be independent" and "be your own person" has pulled us away from holy vulnerability, thereby pulling us away from peace. The modern-day strength facade has weakened us more than strengthened us. We are designed to be dependent on God and healthily dependent on one another. We will discuss this more in the chapter on loneliness, but for now, keep in mind that the independent strength mantra is leading us away from peace rather than toward it.

Because we are designed to be part of the collective body of Christ, we will struggle to have peace apart from it.

QUESTIONS FOR REFLECTION

1   What keeps you from peace?

2   From the list of tips and tools found in this chapter, what is the first step you will take toward finding peace?

CHAPTER 8

LONELINESS

LONELINESS DOES NOT play favorites. It functions like an unwelcome visitor who chooses to take up residence in your home. Loneliness doesn't regard relationship status as an obstacle—the number of people in your life does not deter its presence. Loneliness often prefers a crowd because then it can hide undetected.

New mothers, exhausted, having time only for their babes, feel alone in the unknown newness.

Men, trying to be supportive of their families, find it difficult to build friendships as it takes time away from their God-given priorities.

The single man or woman, engaged in all things social, goes home to an empty house, sometimes wishing for someone to come home to.

There's the wife, feeling unable to talk to anyone about her frustrated marriage.

The child, often quiet, feeling lost and misunderstood.

Loneliness can come to us all.

LONGING FOR CONNECTION

I can recall multiple times in life when I longed for deep friendships. As a child and young adult, I was a hopeless romantic. In my head, I lived in the stories of the books that I read. There was one thing that most of the stories pointed to: being known by and important to someone.

Growing up in a military family, we moved around a lot, so friendships would come and go. They were mostly seasonal and friendships of proximity. Once we moved (these were the days before keeping up with people via social media), I usually did not see or hear from those friends again, at least not consistently.

I longed to have a rich friendship like David and Jonathan in the Bible. To be so deeply connected with a person—sharing values, insights, and growing together. It was my prayer for years.

And then it happened. I gained that type of friend, and I was so grateful. Those are still cherished memories. But due to circumstances beyond my friend's and my control, a point came when we were no longer able to be close friends.

So I prayed again. And again. I've had so many "best friends" over the years that I have questioned my effectiveness as a friend. In reality, a lot of the changes had to do with relocating.

I know what it is like to be lonely. I know what it is like to be surrounded by people and not feel fully seen or known. In the church I am in now, it took eight years before I formed deep friendships with other women. A large part of that is because I was (and am) consistently an outlier. Initially, I was single and the only one my age who was. Then I got married in my thirties. And while most people my age have teenagers or kids in college, at the time of this writing, I have a six-year-old and a three-year-old. My peers' life circumstances tend to be very different from mine.

My church has been with me through a lot. They are truly like family, and I love them deeply. But it took a while to find close friends.

There is one thing that I haven't mentioned before now that may be helpful to note. Because of my often-serious demeanor and my job as a counselor, some people find me intimidating. These have been isolating components in my life at times. It's not anyone's fault, and I certainly try my best not to come across in an aloof or intimidating fashion. But it still happens.

What finally broke the cloud of loneliness for me was confessing at a women's retreat that I felt lonely. The ladies there were women I respected. They were trustworthy. I genuinely desired better connection with them. So I took the risk and confessed my heart.

The response was warmth, kindness, and some sorrow over not knowing I felt that way. Most of the women who were there that day have sought to be more intentional in friendship with me, and I with them. Do we talk all the time or get to spend a lot of time together? No, our schedules don't tend to give us those opportunities. But when we do spend time together, the fellowship is sweet and meaningful.

Because of that retreat, another woman who has become one of my closest friends felt the freedom to draw near. At the risk of sounding strange, I had admired her for a while and desired to become good friends. I didn't know she felt similarly. Now she is the friend I call if I need prayer, encouragement, or someone to challenge me. She entertains my crazy ideas, does not hesitate to lovingly speak truth into my life, and was by my side on two of the hardest days: the day we found out about my husband's tumor and the day of his surgery. I am so grateful for her friendship.

DEFINING LONELINESS

If you ask multiple people who have experienced loneliness how they would describe it, you will likely get just as many different answers. While each person's encounters with loneliness may vary, common themes emerge. Author and counselor Dr. Mark Mayfield defines loneliness in this way: "The state of being unseen or unnoticed relationally, mentally, emotionally, physically, or spiritually. It can be driven by lack of purpose or meaning, relationship, and/or identity and is marked by a deep sense of hopelessness."[34]

Keep in mind that there can be fluctuating levels of loneliness. The intensity may not be as strong as feeling hopeless. The feeling may be more of an internal ache that is not easily soothed. But it's important to understand that this ache points to the way we were designed.

Genesis 2:18 says, "Then the Lord God said, 'It is not good that the man should be alone; I will make him a helper fit for him.'" We were created for connection. Loneliness points to a part of our design that is not being nourished. In the same way that hunger pangs reveal the need to eat and thirst reveals the need for hydration, loneliness reveals the need for others.

When we are known and accepted with all our vulnerabilities in mind, we gain a sense of belonging. Feeling emotionally safe with someone is vital to healing. We reflect our Creator when we are in healthy relationships with others, which, in turn, allows us to be more vulnerable.

Genesis 1:27 says, "So God created man in his own image, in the image of God he created him; male and female he created them." Part of being created in God's image is our desire to be known. God has always been a relational God, even before creation. He is literally three-in-one. As a triune God, all parts know each other. The Father knows what the Son is doing (Matt. 11:27). The Father knows the mind of the Spirit (Rom. 8:26-27). Jesus even states, "I and the Father are one" (John 10:30).

We are created to reflect the triune nature of God. Living a life of complete solitude is contrary to our very makeup. Our basic need is to know God. And part of knowing him means getting to know the body of Christ and learning how to be a part of it, which we'll talk about a little later in this chapter.

There is also a difference between feeling lonely and choosing to be alone. The two do not equal one another. The Gospel writers specifically point out that Jesus made time and space to be alone, without his followers. Being alone did not mean he was lonely. He was content in either capacity.

JESUS AND LONELINESS: JOHN 16:31-32

John 16:31-32 says, "Jesus answered them, 'Do you now believe? Behold, the hour is coming, indeed it has come, when you will be scattered, each to his own home, and will leave me alone. Yet I am not alone, for the Father is with me.'"

Was Jesus lonely as we get lonely? That is a very good question, and I cannot guarantee the answer. We know he purposely got alone in times of grief and when he desired to pray, but neither of those speaks to the state of loneliness. We know Jesus predicted that he would be left alone by his disciples (John 16:31-32). But in that same prediction, he also said he is never truly alone because the Father is with him.

So, for the purposes of this chapter and in an effort to promote biblical accuracy, we will look at the *elements* of loneliness that Jesus experienced, while not necessarily saying he was in a full state of loneliness. We know he was betrayed, which is its own type of loneliness. We know he was physically left alone by his friends and disciples. We know he purposely sought to be alone in grief (see chapter 3). He was, however, never in a state of hopelessness, as our definition of loneliness indicates that we sometimes experience.

JESUS AND BEING ALONE

Jesus chose to be alone. Why? Often these scenes are depicted in Scripture as purposeful times of solitude. He got alone to pray and commune with his Father. These were times he could rest and experience restoration in the fellowship of God. Let's take a look at a few examples:

- "And after he had dismissed the crowds, he went up on the mountain by himself to pray. When evening came, he was there alone." (Matt. 14:23)
- "And rising very early in the morning, while it was still dark, he departed and went out to a desolate place, and there he prayed." (Mark 1:35)
- "Now it happened that as he was praying alone, the disciples were with him." (Luke 9:18a)

The last one is interesting as it says Jesus was alone *and* the disciples were there. Even with other people present, he still found a way to pray alone.

There is so much we can learn from Christ's example of spending time alone! If you have more alone time than you'd prefer, may I suggest using some of that time to do as Jesus did and pray? You may be on the opposite end of this spectrum and struggle to find any alone time. What could be slightly adjusted to offer a modicum of time alone? There are no requirements or restrictions. The goal is simply to pray.

Whether you choose to be alone or you find yourself alone more than you'd like to be, moments of solitude allow us to discover a unique dependency on God.

It is good for us to choose to be alone so that we can face our thoughts, quiet our minds, and seek contentment in Christ. Faith can grow through receiving comfort from our Creator.

What if we found ourselves in a quiet, holy place, our attention completely captured by Christ? Would our affections change? Would our longings shift? Would we find peace, hope, and joy that only he can provide?

What if we were confident that the Father is with us always? What about the Holy Spirit? Jesus? What if, by fully believing that God is with us always, we take comfort in his care, we find friendship with him, and we rest our souls in a love and peace like no other? What if he truly became the primary focus of our heart's desire?

JESUS AND BETRAYAL

For three years, Jesus walked closely with twelve men. He taught them (Mark 4:34). He healed a disciple's mother (Mark 1:29). He empowered them for ministry (Mark 2:14-15; Matt. 10:1). They witnessed him cast out demons, heal deformities and sickness, and raise people from the dead.

Then, on a day when Jesus could have used his friends and beloved disciples for support, they ran. One betrayed him, and one denied even knowing him:

- "And he came the third time and said to them, 'Are you still sleeping and taking your rest? It is enough; the hour has come. The Son of Man is betrayed into the hands of sinners. Rise, let us be going; see, my betrayer is at hand.'" (Mark 14:41-42)
- "While he was still speaking, there came a crowd, and the man called Judas, one of the twelve, was leading them. He drew near to Jesus to kiss him, but Jesus said to him, 'Judas, would you betray the Son of Man with a kiss?'" (Luke 22:47-48)
- "And they all left him and fled." (Mark 14:50)
- "Now Simon Peter was standing and warming himself. So they said to him, 'You also are not one of his disciples, are you?' He denied it and said, 'I am not.'" (John 18:25)

Can you imagine being wrongfully accused of a crime punishable by death and then having all your friends desert you? That sounds unbearable.

We know that, at some point after running away, John reappeared on the scene because Jesus spoke to him while on the cross (John 19:26-27). And Peter followed along at a distance, though he verbally denied knowing Jesus three times (John 18:17, 25-27).

Jesus knows the grief and sorrow of betrayal all too well.

My guess is you know it too.

So do I.

Last year alone, I encountered three betrayals in the span of three months. One case involved lying, one leaving, and the other deception. My heart and mind swirled in and out of grief, anger, and deep sorrow. I wanted to scream, cry, protect myself, and right all the wrongs, which I knew I could not do.

The aftermath of betrayal is like weathering a storm. Emotions feel chaotic. For me, the desire to run, hide, and escape consistently bubbles to the surface. All the duties and demands of life continue while you now carry this heavy sorrow. It hurts.

Often, after being betrayed, it can be hard to trust again—with anyone. Your heart is tender and feels bruised, if not bludgeoned.

The way I see it, there are two options for responding to betrayal: (1) Become bitter and isolate yourself out of fear, or (2) seek healing, forgiveness, and potentially restoration (when appropriate). The latter must be pursued with much wisdom or else greater hurt can transpire.

If you are currently experiencing the pain of betrayal, please be kind to yourself. It is such a devastating experience that can lead to anger, irritability, anxiety, depression, and loneliness. Know that that person (or group of people) does not define who you are in Christ. Grieve the loss. Seek healing as soon as you are able. Try not to walk through this hurt alone. When we open ourselves up to healing, we can open ourselves up to responding like Jesus.

After Jesus rose from the grave, he appeared to his disciples. He did not shame them or rebuke them. He showed them who he was and what he had done—namely, he overcame death. He defeated the one who ultimately betrayed him—Satan.

He also gave Peter the opportunity for restoration. Peter denied Jesus verbally three times. In kindness and love, Jesus gave Peter the opportunity to express his love the exact number of times that he had denied him. What stunning grace!

As you are considering how to apply this, keep a few things in mind. Judas did not come to Jesus for forgiveness and restoration. He went back to his conspirators instead. Peter was sorrowful and acknowledged what he had done prior to the restoration after the resurrection. After the third denial and upon hearing the rooster crow (as Jesus predicted), Luke 22:62 says this of Peter: "And he went out and wept bitterly."

Jesus offers reconciliation, and our response is repentance. But he does not force it.

Similarly for us, we cannot force the person who betrayed us to repent and change. The conviction and contrition can only come from the Holy Spirit's work in that person's life.

Unfortunately, being betrayed is a part of living in a fallen world with fallen people. I do not say that nonchalantly but for the purpose of recognizing that we must learn how to grieve and respond to betrayal.

For our responses to reflect Christ, they need to reflect grace, forgiveness, and wisdom. I stress wisdom because it is not always healthy for all relationships to be restored on this side of heaven. Repentance must be part of restoration.

I am not going to lie—doing the work to heal is hard. But it is worth it. There will be days you do not want to face the pain. I understand. Ask the Lord to comfort you and carry you through those days. One of the maddening realizations of this process is knowing you did not have control. Someone else caused all the pain, and now you are the one having to work through it. I do not like that part of it, but to this I would say do not allow any pain to be wasted. God can and will use it for good and his glory. The cross is not the end of the story. The resurrection is!

LONELINESS IN THE CHURCH

Though the church was meant to be a place of comfort and connection, unfortunately it has become a place where many people have experienced loneliness or betrayal. Very few people escape what is commonly referred to as "church hurt." Even writing that statement pains my heart. These hurts can take many forms: physical, verbal, sexual, or spiritual abuse (the latter of which often looks like using Scripture to manipulate someone for personal gain or control); ignoring problems and concerns; and a feeling of being overlooked or not considered. That is just to name a few.

While there is no excuse for this hurt, there is a reason: We are humans trying to hold ourselves and others to a perfect standard that is impossible to meet. We fear being vulnerable, so we hide behind power and control. We struggle to respect others and desire to be respected at the same time.

Please remember that the church should only and ever be about one person: Christ. When he is not the center of the function and focus of the church, then congregations can fall prey to destruction. Additionally, when he is not our focus, we can easily get distracted by the failures of man.

Ultimately, however, the church is where we are meant to grow as believers and find sanctification, strength for life, and respite for our weary souls. We have the privilege of reminding each other of truth. We have the honor of worshiping together. We have the opportunity to be encouraged by one another's faith. When the body of Christ comes together and functions as Jesus leads, we can flourish rather than falter. We can do so much more for the kingdom together than apart. We do not have to be forever alone in this life when we are unified with other believers in Christ.

Ephesians 4:15-16 speaks of the body of Christ this way: "Rather, speaking the truth in love, we are to grow up in every way into him who is the head, into Christ, from whom the whole body, joined and held together by every joint with which it is equipped, when each part is working properly, makes the body grow so that it builds itself up in love."

Despite our struggles, the church is still the best place for connection and fighting loneliness. When you can link arms with other believers who are consistently seeking Christ, then you have a solid foundation for building friendships. When we trust Christ with our reputations, we can let our guard down and be vulnerable with people who have proven themselves trustworthy. Vulnerability in an environment of compassion promotes safety, healing, and connection. Is it a risk? Yes. But sometimes you have to take the risk to be vulnerable (with trustworthy people) in order to find the relationships you are looking for. The alternative is to stay isolated and lonely.

COMMON MISCONCEPTIONS

There are a few misconceptions about people, the body of Christ, and life in general that foster an environment of loneliness. I want to briefly bring awareness to these areas, because where there is awareness, there is the ability to help safeguard against lies of the enemy. Here are five common misconceptions that contribute to loneliness:

1   **I don't want to be a burden to anyone.** This is a lie of self-protection and deception. The interpretation can be read,

I don't want to be vulnerable and face someone not liking or accepting me as a result.

Lean into what Scripture says: "Bear one another's burdens, and so fulfill the law of Christ" (Gal. 6:2). This verse primarily refers to the burden of temptation. Romans 12:15 says, "Rejoice with those who rejoice, weep with those who weep." We are to encourage, challenge, and participate with one another in our emotions. We were never meant to live in isolation.

2   **If I were more sociable, I wouldn't be so lonely.** The issue with this thought, while there may be an element of truth to it, is that sociability does not guarantee connection. Most people would say that I am a rather social person. But I have gone through personal bouts of loneliness, regardless of how many friends I had. It is not about sociability, but it is all about vulnerability and connectedness.

3   **A relationship will solve my loneliness.** Relationships—familial, friendly, or romantic—can help with loneliness and ideally should. But unless there is reciprocated vulnerability and trust, the loneliness will linger. Do not expect one person to alleviate your loneliness. That puts you and that person in a dangerous position that could lead to an unhealthy imbalance where you seek to meet each other's needs to the extent that others (and God) may be neglected.

4   **Loneliness is always bad.** I do not think anyone would say that the feeling of loneliness is comfortable. On the contrary, it often gives us a deep sense of ache, emptiness, and isolation. It dances on the edge of darkness, desiring to pull us into depressive thinking. So, in that respect, yeah, loneliness is

not fun. However, it provides opportunity. It is a signal that we have a need that's not being met, which can cause us to turn to God for comfort. We can turn to him for provision, and we can implore him to meet our need in an earthly, tangible way too. We can also seek to be more intentional with developing relationships in our lives.

5   **That person must feel so lonely because they are alone.** My husband is an excellent case study for this point. He was set on being a bachelor for the rest of his life and was rather content with that decision. Let's just say that God changed his mind on that one. But ultimately, he didn't struggle with loneliness on a regular basis. There were times he felt lonely, but it wasn't enough of an issue for him to worry about it or dwell on it.

Are there any other misconceptions you would include? This is not an exhaustive list, and I do not dare claim to cover every facet of loneliness here. I hope that by calling our attention to these misconceptions, we will have a better understanding of what we or others may be facing.

SPEAK TRUTH

Loneliness is a tricky feeling. Because it is a reflection of a need, it is not always easily changed. You can remind yourself of truth to keep you anchored during times of loneliness, but it won't necessarily change the *feeling* of loneliness. At least not immediately.

The desire to know and be known, to love and be loved, to accept and be accepted is deeply ingrained in us. Loneliness reflects a longing for something good.

Loneliness does not have to be a "bad" experience. At the risk of sounding trite, let me encourage you by saying loneliness can point you toward a deeper communion with God. Lack of something (or someone) often causes a person to do one of two things: accuse the Creator or seek him for provision. Going to God for comfort out of a position of loneliness can bring peace and encouragement to your longing soul. Remember that he truly is the One who will never leave you or turn his back on you. He always loves you. He delights in you.

Another practical step you can take when you're feeling lonely is to pray Scripture. So many people of faith we admire from the Bible spoke God's truths back to him. It is not as though God forgot what he said. But the person was remembering what God said and vocalizing it before him, sometimes out of desperate pleas for his mercy and relief. Let's explore a few verses together that have specific comforts to offer when we are experiencing loneliness.

Zephaniah 3:17 says, "The Lord your God is in your midst, a mighty one who will save; he will rejoice over you with gladness; he will quiet you by his love; he will exult over you with loud singing." This is our hope in the midst of loneliness—this feeling does not diminish the hope we have in God. It does not remove us from his presence or keep us from experiencing his love and affection. This verse reminds us he is with us, he will calm ("quiet") us, and he delights in us. I pray this speaks truth to your weary soul if loneliness is something you are currently experiencing.

Another verse to remember is Psalm 34:18: "The Lord is near to the brokenhearted and saves the crushed in spirit." Did you catch that? He is *near*. In seasons of hurt, longing, or heartbreak, we need to remember that God is very near and cares deeply for us.

There was a time in my life when my heart had been shattered to a point where I was utterly devastated. I needed a life change, so I decided to go to college. I was twenty-one. Since I was so emotionally raw and needing to recover, I was hesitant about friendships and relationships.

God pointed me to Psalm 101:6 and this became my prayer: "I will look with favor on the faithful in the land, that they may dwell with me; he who walks in the way that is blameless shall minister to me." I asked God to show me the faithful of the land. To this day, the people he brought me during that time are some of my best and most cherished friends (even if we don't get to talk as much now).

As we wrap up our conversation on loneliness, I want to offer a few other Scriptures to pray through or ponder:

- "The Lord is my shepherd; I shall not want. He makes me lie down in green pastures. He leads me beside still waters. He restores my soul. He leads me in paths of righteousness for his name's sake. Even though I walk through the valley of the shadow of death, I will fear no evil; for you are with me; your rod and your staff, they comfort me." (Ps. 23:1-4)
- "The friendship of the Lord is for those who fear him, and he makes known to them his covenant." (Ps. 25:14)
- "Turn to me and be gracious to me, for I am lonely and afflicted." (Ps. 25:16)
- "O Lord, you have searched me and known me! You know when I sit down and when I rise up; you discern my thoughts from afar. You search out my path and my lying down and are acquainted with all my ways." (Ps. 139:1-3)
- "'For the mountains may depart and the hills be removed, but my steadfast love shall not depart from you, and my covenant of peace shall not be removed,' says the Lord, who has compassion on you." (Isa. 54:10)
- "And behold, I am with you always, to the end of the age." (Matt. 28:20b)
- "Let us then with confidence draw near to the throne of grace, that we may receive mercy and find grace to help in time of need." (Heb. 4:16)

This is my prayer for you: that these verses would help you draw near to God and allow him to comfort you through any loneliness you may be walking through.

QUESTIONS FOR REFLECTION

1   How would you define loneliness?

2   Which misconception surprised you most, and why?

3   Do you have anyone in your life who has proven them-
    selves safe and trustworthy whom you can reach out to
    and risk sharing about your loneliness? If not, where are
    some places you can go to begin looking for someone
    like this?

4   Even if it's only for five minutes, when is an upcoming
    time that you could "get alone" to pray?

CHAPTER 9

JOY

IN THIS SEASON for my family, when we have faced many trials and really difficult challenges, I find myself revisiting the concept of joy. Most days lately, I feel like I am trudging through as the aftermath of my husband's surgery, the pressures of running a business, and trying to love people well take their toll on my soul. This week, I am trying to remind myself to pursue joy through something simple: music.

I used to listen to a lot of music. Now I go through spurts of what I listen to. Often, if it's not "productive" (i.e., a book, podcast, etc.), I don't listen to it as much. I am trying to change that because music revitalizes my spirit like almost nothing else. Lately, I have been introducing my girls to music I grew up with and dancing around with them as we listen. I have always been a person who tends to lean more toward the serious side of life, but as the Lord has been reminding me to consider the importance of joy, I've challenged myself to do something each day to make my girls smile. Dancing with them as we listen to music I love has been such a fun way to do that. These moments together remind me of what joy was designed to do—how these little moments of celebration lighten the load, even if only for the span of a single song.

There is so much confusion surrounding *joy*, this one little word that is supposed to be lovely and life-giving. How many times have you heard, particularly from Christians, that there is a difference between *joy* and *happiness*? If that is the case, then what *is* the difference? Usually, this separation is a well-intended attempt to distinguish between the temporary pleasures of this world and the deeper joy that comes from following Christ. But I believe that the two words are more closely associated than what has been touted. If you were to do a study on the Hebrew and Greek words that translate to *joy*, you would find very similar definitions. So why have so many tried to separate the two?

Telling a person to "just be happy," "choose joy," or "rejoice always" falls flat in times of hardship. Those are not soothing words to a weary soul, because they gloss over the present pain. As we discussed regarding grief and distress, pain needs to be acknowledged and processed before it can heal. Without that, these joy directives can come across as discouraging statements of failure. The recipient is left feeling angry, confused, or even more sad because they think they cannot respond to difficult circumstances in a "godly" way.

And this is how my desire to explore the emotions of Jesus came to be. I saw too many people trying to perfect their emotions and responses to grievous circumstances instead of responding with the genuine grief and pain that were warranted. All because someone somewhere told them they needed to be joyful no matter what. This disproportionate focus on joy is part of why I've saved the discussion on this oft-misunderstood emotion for last. Joy is important for us to explore and understand, especially as we put it in its proper place alongside the array of emotions we've studied so far.

I appreciate Margaret Feinberg's definition of joy as "A spectrum of emotions, actions, and responses that includes gladness, cheer, happiness, merriment, delighting, dancing, shouting, exulting, rejoicing, laughing, playing, brightening, blessing and being blessed, taking pleasure in and being well pleased."[35] That pretty much sums up every definition in Scripture too.

We need joy. Joy is a gift, ever accessible to the one who believes in Christ. God knows we are too frail and weak on our own to be able to fight the battles of life and not grow weary, tired, and discouraged, or at times, even depressed, anxious, and despondent.

But God.

He gives the gift of joy to lift our focus from the harshness of life—if only for a short reprieve—because we need glimpses of heaven. We need rest. We need life spoken back to our souls.

Imagine being stranded in the middle of the ocean. Magnificent sea creatures you have admired in movies and books are now too close for comfort, presenting great danger. You are determined to survive, but you don't know how long you will last. You see a large buoy, offering relief from swimming. Now you can float. Now you have something that pulls you out of the water for a time. But you are still in the middle of the ocean.

A day passes, and you see a small boat in the distance. The driver pulls you aboard. Again, more relief.

The boat driver takes you ashore. Only now, you are in a different country where you don't speak the language. While there is physical relief, you are still a long way from home.

It takes days, weeks, and even months to get out of this harrowing ordeal. All you have been able to focus on is how to survive, how to get home, and how to end the horrible nightmare.

In the harsh realities of life, joy comes in like the buoy, the boat, and any helper along the way. Joy gets you home. Joy reminds you that life is not all about what you are going through. It points to the hope you have in waiting for the goodness to come.

Joy is like a warm light shining in the darkness and pushing it away. Joy speaks life to weary bones. Joy draws you to hope and hope to joy.

JOY IN THE OLD TESTAMENT

The Hebrew words for "joy" (*simchah, chedwah, rinnah, gil,* and *sason*) are mentioned more than 160 times in the Old Testament. In most of these instances, "joy is closely related to victory over one's enemies."[36] David rejoiced over the recovery of the ark of the covenant (1 Chron. 15:25). Israel and Judah rejoiced over their enemies (2 Chron. 20:27). The Jews of Persia were saved from complete annihilation and their response was to celebrate through feasting and giving gifts, initiating a new holiday of remembrance (Esther 9:22).

Joy reminds us of victory. It is a vibrant reminder that the grave is not what we were created for. Pondering the impact of the resurrecting power of Jesus Christ over sin, death, and hell, points us to victory. It points us to joy.

Joy is also commonly used in expressions of worship. The psalmists use the term multiple times to respond to the magnificence, power, and goodness of God. These songs emphasize that God is deserving of joy-filled praise. I particularly like Psalm 149 and the thought of singing in bed: "Let the godly exult in glory; let them sing for joy on their beds" (Ps. 149:5).

What would happen if tonight when you go to bed, you start singing a song of worship to God? Perhaps you are like me and the challenge would be more appropriate for waking up in the morning (I am *not* a morning person). Usually, we can fight our way through the day, keeping heaviness at bay. But the weight of the day often catches up with us at night as we attempt a fitful rest. This is another area many (including me) need to see victory in.

Praising God reminds us of the power that he has, the promises he has fulfilled, and the work he is doing. I have challenged people to praise God before going to sleep rather than expressing concerns through prayer. Prayer is wonderful and vital to our spiritual well-being. But praying about the concerns on your heart and mind just before trying to sleep usually keeps those worries circulating in your mind, rather than helping you to relinquish them. What if you praise God before you go to sleep—either instead of praying or after praying? I encourage you to try this and see how it begins to impact your sleep.

Both the Old and New Testaments point to joy's connection to gratitude. Gratitude for victory. Gratitude for deliverance. Gratitude for salvation.

JESUS AND JOY

Have you ever noticed that the Gospels do not say anything about Jesus laughing or smiling? Yet because he was fully God and fully man, we can assume that he did. Part of the human experience is to laugh and smile. Were we to go through life without cracking a smile, we would be miserable, unhappy people.

While joy is not an emotion that we see explicitly expressed by Jesus in the Gospels, it was very much his purpose. His reason for joy may be slightly different than ours. Hebrews 12:2 says of Jesus, "… who for the joy that was set before him endured the cross, despising the shame, and is seated at the right hand of God." That joy was a restored relationship with his people. That joy involved victory over his enemies. That joy was *us*. B.B. Warfield describes Jesus's joy this way: "Joy he had: but it was not the shallow joy of mere pagan delight in living, nor the delusive joy of a hope destined to failure; but the deep exultation of a conqueror setting captives free."[37]

Luke 10:21 supports the claim that we are the reason for Christ's joy, saying, "In that same hour he rejoiced in the Holy Spirit and said, 'I thank you, Father, Lord of heaven and earth, that you have hidden these things from the wise and understanding and revealed them to little children; yes, Father, for such was your gracious will.'"

Jesus wants us to know him. He rejoiced over those who understood and believed the truth of the kingdom of heaven.

Not only would Jesus have experienced joy, but he is also our source of joy. Sometimes I wonder how much our modern view of the self impacts our ability to experience joy. We are often more concerned with our own desires than with sanctification. We are quick to look for relief and comfort in the material things of this world instead of Jesus. We endlessly scroll through social media or watch countless hours of television, intrigued and drawn in by someone else's story. We are created for story, but we're in danger of missing out on the one God has for us by being so distracted by the stories we consume. Our affections are misappropriated. We think we don't have time to delight in Jesus, but in reality, we have pushed away the opportunities to find joy in him.

We also think so little of our sin and who we are in the flesh that we seldom grasp the magnitude of Jesus's sacrifice. If we paused to repent, to recognize that our sin is great, we would be more open, humble, and grateful for the fact that the grace of Jesus is so much greater. It is from that place of humility, repentance, and gratitude that I believe we can begin delighting in Jesus, thereby receiving joy.

ABIDING JOY

Jesus speaks of his disciples having the opportunity to know full joy. What must they—we—do to find this joy? Abide in him. In John 15:11, Jesus says, "These things I have spoken to you, that my joy may be in you, and that your joy may be full." Just before this, he challenged his disciples to abide in him, connecting to him as branches are connected to the vine. Darlene Wilkinson defines abiding in this way: "It means to stay, to remain, to continue in fellowship with. In that word, Jesus was calling His disciples to strengthen and enlarge

their connection to Him, the Vine—to *be with Him* more and more."[38]
We are to be that interconnected with Jesus.

What does it look like to stay connected with Jesus? I believe that, practically speaking, there are a multitude of ways we can abide with him. Let's discuss just a few of those possibilities.

One easily accessible option is to think about Jesus. Think about his character, his sacrifice, his humility. Think about what you long to know about him. Think about how it feels to spend time with him. And my favorite: think about how he experienced emotion.

Hopefully, thinking about Jesus and wondering about him will lead to exploration. Reading Scripture is a great way to abide in him, and he challenges us to have his *words* abide in us as well (John 15:7). Finding a specific verse or passage to mull over for a day or a week can bring your attention to Jesus throughout the day. Write it on a mirror, put it on a sticky note on your desk, or text it to a friend.

Another way to abide with Jesus is to talk to him. What would it be like if you thought of Jesus as being with you all day, wherever you go, willing to converse with you at any time? He *is* with you. You *do* have constant access to him. You can't abide with him much more than *all the time*.

It is really hard to access joy if we are not willing to engage with its source—Jesus.

FRUIT OF THE SPIRIT

Joy is an emotion that can bubble up when your heart is sparked by a thought, memory, person, or other exciting stimuli. And it can be pursued, focused on, and invited in. It is also unique in that it is a fruit of the Spirit.

If the fruit listed in Galatians 5:22-23 were ranked in importance by the order in which they appear, joy would be in the top two! It comes second only to love. Now, I don't believe that the passage is meant to be ranked, but all of these characteristics are important. We can't claim to believe in the Lord Jesus Christ as our Savior and also ignore the power the Holy Spirit provides. It is through the Holy Spirit that we have "love, joy, peace, patience, kindness, goodness, faithfulness, gentleness, self-control" (Gal. 5:22-23).

I don't know about you, but all of those are incredibly difficult to experience when I am functioning in my natural flesh or leaning into worldly comforts instead of the encouragement of the Holy Spirit. But we have been given access to all the fruit, all the time. God will never say "no" in response to a request to help us be more _____ (fill in the blank with your fruit of choice). We can expect that the fruit will flow when we give attention to the Spirit.

Keep in mind that as a fruit of the Spirit, joy comes from God. Sin does not produce joy. It inhibits it. Sin may produce pleasure for a period of time, but not joy. Joy is rooted in Jesus. Joy is life-giving, whereas sin leads to death—emotional, physical, and spiritual death. I say this because I want to encourage you to not mix up a pursuit of joy with a pursuit of selfish desire. The very next verse speaks to this: "And those who belong to Christ Jesus have crucified the flesh with its passions and desires" (Gal. 5:24). Earlier, Paul says the "desires of the flesh are against the Spirit, and the desires of the Spirit are against the flesh" (Gal. 5:17a). Joy is one of the desires of the Holy Spirit. What may be contradicting joy in your life?

JOY AND COMMUNITY

Joy is mentioned more than sixty times in the New Testament, and we seldom see it expressed without a connection to other people. The writers of the epistles refer to their audiences as arbiters of joy in their lives. When they merely *think* of the people they are writing to, they have joy. Paul has "much joy and comfort" from the love and ministry of Philemon (Philem. 1:7). Titus has joy "because his spirit has been refreshed by you all" (2 Cor. 7:13). Paul called the Philippian church his "joy and crown" (Phil. 4:1). Paul writes to the church at Thessalonica, declaring them to be his and his companions' "glory and joy" (1 Thess. 2:20).

Joy was not intended to be an isolated experience. Even the promptings to rejoice were spoken to entire groups of people in Scripture. Churches and nations were collectively challenged to consider joy.

Joy-filled people are not necessarily that way because of their personalities or positions in life. Instead, they are typically surrounded by people who encourage them in faith, love, truth, hope, and joy. They are not isolated.

Put a usually joyful person in isolation for an extended period, and their joy may begin to wane. Like Paul, if that person wishes to strengthen her heart, she may meditate on all the encouragers in her life. Receiving letters of encouragement from others would be another source of joy for her.

Joy is found in community. Spirits are revived when true connection is made. But you have to be willing to look for and receive that connection.

We have to pursue joy. I wish joy were a more natural aspect of our makeup, but it isn't. It is, however, a natural part of the *Holy Spirit*. It is a fruit of the *Spirit*. It is certainly not a fruit of our flesh. And the flesh has tainted our understanding and application of joy in life by deceiving us into thinking that it is an emotion of indulgence and selfishness, unencumbered by pain.

This week, I was faced with the decision to choose joy over what I felt like doing. I had a moment of extreme fear that completely wiped me out emotionally and physically. I was drained. The thought of going to spend time with people—even though they are my life-giving people—was exhausting to consider. I wanted to curl up in bed and be left alone. (I can easily retreat to "withdraw mode" at any point. It is my natural go-to.) Instead, I remembered exactly what I have been studying—that joy is connected to community. And I knew that if I spent time with my friends, particularly discussing Scripture, I would be revived. So I made myself go (sans makeup).

It worked. I felt better. Pursuing joy with others helped reset my body and refreshed my spirit. Choosing to find joy and fight for joy is worth it, friend.

PRACTICE JOY

You may be in the throes of depression, grief, deep pain, or anxiety. If so, this chapter may seem a little irritating. I get it. When I was severely depressed, I did not want anyone talking to me about joy. Please know that this discussion is not intended to be a quick fix or a complete solution to your pain. The intention has been to point us all to the truth by looking at the emotions of Jesus and learning what is available to all of us—even in deep pain.

Joy is one of those emotions that we often get robbed of due to the weight of the burdens we carry. We can forget about joy as we trudge through the heaviness and struggles of life. And while joy is not necessarily something to be forced, I do believe we can foster a better environment for it. It helps if we start by being open to receiving joy.

Part of this openness involves recognizing that joy and sorrow can coexist—they often do. Joy is richer through sorrow. It's more cherished as a result. Keep this in mind, because I think many see joy as the opposite of sorrow or a complete removal of pain. When we view it this way, we miss experiencing the joy that is readily available to us through the Holy Spirit because we are expecting it to look like an absence of hardship rather than a hope that sustains us through it.

We would all greatly benefit from opening our minds and hearts to expressions of joy. For when we look for joy, will we not also find Jesus?

I want to use the Bible as our playbook for practicing joy. There are some action words connected to expressions of joy that may prove helpful (and, dare I say, fun) to our pursuit of joy. Try them and see which ones lighten your spirit a little (or a lot!):

1. **Sing for joy:** "But let all who take refuge in you rejoice; let them ever sing for joy, and spread your protection over them, that those who love your name may exult in you." (Ps. 5:11)

2. **Shout for joy:** "Be glad in the Lord, and rejoice, O righteous, and shout for joy, all you upright in heart!" (Ps. 32:11)

3. **Clap for joy:** "Let the rivers clap their hands; let the hills sing for joy together." (Ps. 98:8)

4. **Proclaim God's goodness and righteousness:** "They shall pour forth the fame of your abundant goodness and shall sing aloud of your righteousness." (Ps. 145:7)

5. **Ask God:** "Until now you have asked nothing in my name. Ask, and you will receive, that your joy may be full." (John 16:24)

6. **Tell others about Jesus:** "So, being sent on their way... [they were] describing in detail the conversion of the Gentiles, and brought great joy to all the brothers." (Acts 15:3)

7. **Believe the God of hope:** "May the God of hope fill you with all joy and peace in believing, so that by the power of the Holy Spirit you may abound in hope." (Rom. 15:13)

8 **Be hospitable/welcome others:** "So receive him in the Lord with all joy…" (Phil. 2:29a)

A final thought. Through my own experience of deep depression and working with people who also struggle with it, I know that joy often feels elusive, nigh impossible. And if this is where you are right now, I understand. The feeling seems so far off that you can't even remember if you've ever felt joy. I want to say something very lovingly and clearly. Don't be joy-resistant. Don't think that you can't have joy. Joy is possible for *you*. When Jesus is near, so is joy. Consider the following verses as a blessing and prayer for you:

- "[Be] strengthened with all power, according to his glorious might, for all endurance and patience with joy." (Col. 1:11)
- "Blessed be the God and Father of our Lord Jesus Christ! According to his great mercy, he has caused us to be born again to a living hope through the resurrection of Jesus Christ from the dead, to an inheritance that is imperishable, undefiled, and unfading, kept in heaven for you, who by God's power are being guarded through faith for a salvation ready to be revealed in the last time. In this you rejoice, though now for a little while, if necessary, you have been grieved by various trials, so that the tested genuineness of your faith—more precious than gold that perishes though it is tested by fire—may be found to result in praise and glory and honor at the revelation of Jesus Christ. Though you have not seen him, you love him. Though you do not now see him, *you believe in him and rejoice with joy that is inexpressible and filled with glory*, obtaining the outcome of your faith, the salvation of your souls." (1 Pet. 1:3-9, emphasis added)

QUESTIONS FOR REFLECTION

1   Out of the list of actions from the Bible regarding joy, what is the first one you will try?

2   What would your joy list look like? It could include things you enjoy or think you would enjoy, prompts to remind you of joy, or actions that draw your attention to joy.

3   Are you scared to experience joy? If so, what do you think is the reason?

4   What could you do today to choose joy and see victory over the enemy?

CONCLUSION

DO YOU FEEL free yet? It's okay if you don't, though I hope that you are gaining freedom in the way you feel and express emotions. As much as I have studied and worked on these truths in my own life, I still have times when guilt, shame, judgment, or fear do not allow me to feel emotions in the ways I would like. But thankfully, as God continues to remind me of the truth of how he has designed us, I am receiving more and more freedom in this area.

This book has been designed to set you on a path of emotional (and hopefully spiritual) freedom. We have looked at a range of emotions, discussed how they are part of our God-given design, and explored how emotions were or were not experienced by Jesus. But there will always be more to learn. There is always work to be done regarding our beliefs about God and emotions. So, what comes next?

My hope for you is that you won't leave the contents of this book unaddressed in your life but rather that you will grow in your ability to be free to feel and find that to be a holy experience. I pray that your emotions will consistently point you back to God, for we need his truth to guide us at all times and in every season.

Perhaps you will go back to one (or all) of the chapters and look up more verses on that particular emotion. Maybe there was an emotion that was more difficult for you and you need to use the reflection questions to challenge yourself in a specific area. Maybe this whole book has been hard for you and you could use help navigating how to apply it. Can I encourage you to seek out a licensed professional Christian counselor or a well-trained biblical counselor? Such a move is a great step toward emotional freedom.

Remember, emotions are God-given. There is no need to be ashamed for feeling them. If you wouldn't accuse a holy God of being wrong for having emotions, then why do you accuse yourself when you have them? Emotions can either be a holy experience or a fleshly one depending on how you *use* them, not on how you *feel* them.

With that in mind, I pray you feel less ashamed and more alive. I pray you remember daily that God made *all* of you. You are fearfully and wonderfully made.

Through emotions, God has provided our souls with natural, ingrained ways to deal with all the sorrows, sufferings, celebrations, and joys we experience while we tread this earth. For example, tears serve many purposes, seeping out of our eyes in response to many different causes: grief, sadness, joy, pain, anger.

To express the soul is to heal.

To express the soul is to show what is deep within: a person who cares.

To express the soul is to invite connection with others.

To express the soul is to invite connection with your Creator.

Please stop stifling your—or anyone's—emotions. You don't need to be scared of them. Learn how you can use them for God's glory.

Our bodies are not meant to contain all the difficulties or joys of life. The healthy expression of emotions creates room for an abundant life filled with growth, joy, and freedom. It is "For freedom Christ has set us free" (Gal. 5:1a)!

RESPONDING TO EMOTIONS LIKE JESUS

In writing this book, I noticed a theme emerging regarding how Jesus handled emotions. So often we want to do something once we feel an emotion. We want to take action, fix the cause, or move on. However, Jesus's response to other people's emotions and his own was to pursue compassion.

Jesus felt grief, and then he felt compassion. He felt anger, and then he showed compassion. He was betrayed and rejected, but instead of defending himself, he displayed the ultimate act of compassion—sacrificing himself on the cross.

I wonder what it would look like if we pursued compassion in response to our own emotions. This could look like having compassion for ourselves (not shaming ourselves for having emotions in the first place). But even more so, it could look like having compassion for others and intentionally seeking out ways to love those in need.

What if sadness and grief led us to notice when others long for a hug, for someone to care, or for someone to notice them?

What if amazement led us to share with others the wonder of faith?

What if anger led us to seek a way to be kind and gracious to someone in need?

What if distress and anguish led us to comfort and encourage others, to be tender in our interactions with them, and to see needs that no one else may see?

What if we are known by peace rather than turmoil? What if we pursued peace through constant surrender to Jesus, causing others to want to know this benevolent Prince of Peace too?

What if loneliness led us to notice when others are lonely and to invite them into our lives? What if betrayal brought us to a place of solidifying our own trustworthiness?

What if joy led us to attempt to brighten someone's day?

The possibilities are endless. Emotions are not meant to be felt and expressed solely for our own sake (though as we've seen, that is certainly important!). Our experiences with emotions can be used to benefit others as well. They are how we connect, how we empathize, and how we love well. It makes sense, then, that Jesus used them as fuel for compassion.

Like Jesus, may you look at the hurting and be moved with compassion. May you see people as sheep without a shepherd and lead them to the Good Shepherd. May you find creative ways to meet the needs of those who are hungry, thirsty, or hurting. May you know the unique ways God has equipped you as you show mercy.

Like Jesus, may you weep with those who weep and mourn with those who mourn. May you see sadness as a holy opportunity to grieve your suffering and losses. May you see tears as just as valuable as laughter. May you find comfort in Christ as he did with his Father. May you remember that it is Christlike to cry.

Like Jesus, may you marvel at faith. May you marvel at the faith of a child and at anyone whose gaze is fixed on Christ. May you marvel at the faith of someone who has been through seemingly unbearable grievances and yet still believes in God. May you marvel at lack of faith as well.

Like Jesus, may you get angry with the enemy and with death. May you resist being angry at fellow humans and turn your anger toward what Jesus gets angry about: the author of sin and death.

Like Jesus, may you know the heart of the Father more deeply as you experience distress. May you cling to God with hope and faith in his sovereignty through every anguish. May you cry out to the One who saves, delivers, and comforts you. And in your distress, may you find hope in the eternal glory that is and is to come.

Like Jesus, may you know peace by knowing him. May you abide in him so much that peace reigns in your spirit. May you forever look to Jesus for peace that just does not make sense to the onlooker—a peace that "surpasses all understanding" (Phil. 4:7).

Like Jesus, may you know that you are never alone because you have the Father. May your loneliness drive you to connect and risk being vulnerable. May you understand that forgiveness is more powerful than betrayal. May you find deep connection with other believers who represent Christ in your life.

Like Jesus, may you find joy in hope. May you rejoice in the promise of the restoration that is coming. May you feel free to feel joy, knowing it is a God-given relief for your soul.

I pray you find the freedom to feel, knowing your Savior felt too. And still does.

> "And the Word became flesh and dwelt among us, and we have seen his glory, glory as of the only Son from the Father, full of grace and truth." (John 1:14)

> "Therefore, as you received Christ Jesus the Lord, so walk in him, rooted and built up in him and established in the faith, just as you were taught, abounding in thanksgiving." (Col. 2:6-7)

> "Let the word of Christ dwell in you richly, teaching and admonishing one another in all wisdom, singing psalms and hymns and spiritual songs, with thankfulness in your hearts to God. And whatever you do, in word or deed, do everything in the name of the Lord Jesus, giving thanks to God the Father through him." (Col. 3:16-17)

ACKNOWLEDGMENTS

Taking on the endeavor of writing a book was made possible by an amazing group of people. The team at Streamline Books far surpassed my hopes, and they have been so supportive and encouraging. The idea for this book has been percolating for a long time, and I had only begun the preliminary stages of writing when I met Streamline. They have guided me every step of the way, providing structure and deadlines so that this book could happen. They have been patient and kind. Will, thank you for taking a chance on me and for putting the team in place. Your leadership and encouragement have been outstanding. Missy, you are an incredible copyeditor. You asked the hard questions to make the content clear. Thank you for your insight, expertise, and eye for detail. Ruthie, I can't imagine what this process would have been like without you. The Lord knew what my insecurities were regarding this book, and he paired me with the best writing coach/editor/teammate. Through you, God has given me more confidence, made me a better writer, and made this whole process a joy. The intention was to have a coach and yet I gained a friend. I hope this is the first of many projects we do together.

All my clients have had an impact on the contents of this book in various ways through the years. Thank you for having the courage to pursue counseling, and thank you for trusting me with your care. It has been a privilege to watch the redemptive work God is doing in you.

To the Restoring Hope Counseling team, thank you for your patience, for standing in the gaps for me during writing deadlines, and for believing in me, supporting me, and helping me troubleshoot content. You are a reflection of God's goodness and faithfulness in my life. Thank you for believing in me and all my crazy ideas, including writing a book. You truly are family to me, and I am grateful for you every day. I'm thankful I get to work with friends.

My community group through Renewal Church has been by my side from the moment I began praying about this opportunity. We've been through a lot together, haven't we? Thank you for praying this book through to the end. Thank you for upholding our family through some of the most difficult trials in our lives. Because of you, I haven't felt alone. I love our friendship and the way we encourage each other in the gospel. You are an answer to years of prayer.

To my counselor, Julie, you have been such an anchoring point for me. You have taught me about my ability to express emotions and that I don't have to function out of fear, and you continue to encourage me toward doing good work for the glory of God. Thank you for being so consistent in your compassion and care for me and my family. You have carried me through a lot of hard times, and I am incredibly thankful to have you in my life.

To my family, you could have said I was out of my mind for doing this and greatly questioned the timing. You could have completely dismissed the idea. But you didn't. Instead, you believed it was about time that a book happened! Mom, thank you for encouraging me to write from early on in my life. Dad, thank you for always being proud of me. It is a gift to have you as parents.

ACKNOWLEDGMENTS

My husband and girls have been rock stars throughout this process. I had one primary goal and that was to not rob them of much time with me during the writing of this book. Thank you for being patient and gracious with me. Stephen, thank you for consistently being such a supportive husband, willing to challenge me when needed, and for helping me work through some of the theological concepts in this book. Thank you for being open to sharing a part of our story. I admire you and learn so much from you. I love you! Sophie and Josie, I love that you are not afraid to express your emotions and that you love well and hard. I pray that the truths of this book will be instilled in you as you learn and grow. You girls are amazing, and Mommy loves you very much!

Oh precious Jesus, I pray I have regarded you, your Word, and your emotions well. Thank you for continuously teaching me, for sending me on my own journey of emotional discovery, and for providing peace throughout the writing of this book. Thank you for challenging me to get out of my comfort zone and take this risk. Thank you for the clients you send my way. Thank you for the grace you give for all my imperfections. Thank you for being my Redeemer and Savior. Thank you for having emotions so that we can better relate to you and get a glimpse of what it looks like when holiness meets humanity.

ABOUT THE AUTHOR

Holly Randle Spiars, MDiv, LPC-S, is a graduate of the New Orleans Baptist Theological Seminary and a licensed professional counselor and supervisor. She is the founder and director of Restoring Hope Counseling, LLC, a Christian group counseling practice in the Upstate of South Carolina. Holly is passionate about helping people embrace their God-given design, and that includes emotions. She seeks to guide others toward hope and healing through acknowledging the pains of the soul and embracing the comfort of Christ. She resides in South Carolina with her husband and two daughters.

ENDNOTES

1   Dane Ortlund, *Gentle and Lowly: The Heart of Christ for Sinners and Sufferers* (Wheaton, IL: Crossway, 2020), 73-74.

2   *The International Standard Bible Encyclopedia*, rev. ed., ed. Geoffrey W. Bromiley et al., vol. 4, *Q-Z* (Grand Rapids, MI: Eerdmans Publishing Company, 1988), under "self-control."

3   *The Lexham Bible Dictionary*, ed. John D. Barry et al. (Bellingham, WA: Lexham Press, 2016), under "soul."

4   Matthew A. Elliot, *Faithful Feelings: Rethinking Emotion in the New Testament* (Grand Rapids, MI: Kregel Academic, 2006), 78-79.

5   "Psalms Explorer," Logos (software), 2014.

6   "Compassion Definition & Meaning," Merriam-Webster, accessed March 5, 2024, https://www.merriam-webster.com/dictionary/compassion.

7   Robert C. Roberts, *Spiritual Emotions: A Psychology of Christian Virtues* (Grand Rapids, MI: Eerdmans Publishing Company, 2007), 179-180.

8   Leon Morris, *The Gospel according to Matthew* (Grand Rapids, MI: Eerdmans Publishing Company, 1992), 238-239.

9   Morris, *The Gospel according to Matthew*, 239.

10 "Vagus Nerve," Cleveland Clinic, last reviewed January 11, 2022, https://my.clevelandclinic.org/health/body/22279-vagus-nerve.

11 Deb Dana, *The Polyvagal Theory in Therapy: Engaging the Rhythm of Regulation* (New York, NY: W. W. Norton & Company, 2018), 21.

12 *The International Standard Bible Encyclopedia*, rev. ed., ed. Geoffrey W. Bromiley et al., vol. 1 *A-D* (Grand Rapids, MI: Eerdmans Publishing Company, 1988), 755.

13 "Sadness Definition & Meaning," Merriam-Webster, accessed March 8, 2024, https://www.merriam-webster.com/dictionary/sadness.

14 "Grief Definition & Meaning," Merriam-Webster, accessed March 8, 2024, https://www.merriam-webster.com/dictionary/grief.

15 American Psychiatric Association, *Diagnostic and Statistical Manual of Mental Disorders,* Fifth Edition, Text Revision ed. (Washington, DC: American Psychiatric Association Publishing, 2022), 183.

16 Matthew Henry, *Commentary on the Whole Bible: Genesis to Revelation*, ed. Leslie F. Church (Grand Rapids, MI: Zondervan Publishing House, 1961), 1571.

17 Elisabeth Kübler-Ross is the one who came up with the first five stages of grief through her work with hundreds of terminally ill patients. Later, David Kessler added the sixth one. Their work and research can be found in *On Death and Dying, On Grief and Grieving,* and *Finding Meaning.*

18 "Drug Abuse Statistics," National Center for Drug Abuse Statistics, accessed November 25, 2024, https://drugabusestatistics.org/#:~:text=Substance%20Abuse%20Statistics&text=13.5%25%20of%20Americans%2012%20and,drugs%20within%20the%20last%20year.

19 "Alcohol Use Disorder (AUD) in the United States: Age Groups and Demographic Characteristics," National Institute on Alcohol Abuse and Alcoholism, updated September 2024, https://www.niaaa.nih.gov/alcohols-effects-health/alcohol-topics/alcohol-facts-and-statistics/alcohol-use-disorder-aud-united-states-age-groups-and-demographic-characteristics.

20 "Social Media Addiction Statistics," AddictionHelp.com, last updated November 10, 2024, https://www.addictionhelp.com/social-media-addiction/statistics/.

21 Saya Des Marais, "Technology Addiction Statistics 2024," The Center for Internet & Technology Addiction, accessed December 3, 2024, https://virtual-addiction.com/technology-addiction-statistics-2024/.

22 *Lexham Theological Wordbook*, ed. D. Mangum et al. (Bellingham, WA: Lexham Press, 2014), under "mystery."

23 Elliot, *Faithful Feelings: Rethinking Emotion in the New Testament*, 214.

24 Thought gleaned from a sermon titled "Worship Exalts God (John 2:13-22)" by Stephen Watson at Renewal Church in Anderson, South Carolina, on Sunday, May 12, 2024.

25 *The International Standard Bible Encyclopedia,* under "zeal."

26 B. B. Warfield, *The Emotional Life of Our Lord* (Louisville, KY: GLH Publishing, 2022), 31.

27 Warfield, *The Emotional Life of Our Lord*, 33.

28 Warfield, *The Emotional Life of Our Lord*, 34.

29 American Psychiatric Association, *Diagnostic and Statistical Manual of Mental Disorders,* 183

30 Some scholars discount this portion in Luke as these verses are not included in all of the earliest manuscripts.

31 Craig L. Blomberg, *Matthew* (Nashville, TN: Broadman Press, 1992), 22:395.

32 Channing L. Crisler, *Echoes of Lament and the Christology of Luke* (Sheffield, UK: Sheffield Phoenix Press, 2020), 260.

33 Warfield, *The Emotional Life of Our Lord,* 14.

34 Mark Mayfield, *The Path out of Loneliness: Finding and Fostering Connection to God, Ourselves, and One Another* (Colorado Springs, CO: NavPress, 2021), 24.

35 Margaret Feinberg, *Fight Back With Joy: Celebrate More. Regret Less. Stare Down Your Greatest Fears.* (Brentwood, TN: Worthy Publishing, 2015), 18-19.

36 *The Lexham Bible Dictionary*, ed. John D. Barry et al. (Bellingham, WA: Lexham Press, 2016), under "joy."

37 Warfield, *The Emotional Life of Our Lord*, 45.

38 Darlene Marie Wilkinson, *Secrets of the Vine for Women: Breaking Through to Abundance* (Sisters, OR: Multnomah Publishers, Inc., 2003), 76.

www.ingramcontent.com/pod-product-compliance
Lightning Source LLC
Chambersburg PA
CBHW031529120626
46545CB00005B/2058

* 9 7 9 8 8 9 1 6 5 2 3 2 3 *